"The word retirement i_____ or a cave or some other dark place but the r_____ ...ould be, radically different. This phase of life is three decades long for most people, and it needs careful planning. This planning does take place but only about money. People need to think much more broadly, and this book will help them do just that. Covering not only health but much broader, deeper issues such as purpose, it should be given to everyone approaching retirement to help them ensure it is a renaissance."

Professor Sir Muir Gray
Public Health Pioneer | Author of *Increase Your Brainability— And Reduce Your Risk of Dementia*

"Justin is absolutely right when he suggests that in Britain there is a conspiracy of silence about retirement. In this wonderful book, he breaks the *omertà* which normally shrouds this topic, and asks not only the 'when' of retirement, but also the 'why'."

Rory Sutherland
Vice Chairman at Ogilvy UK | TED Global Speaker | Author of *Alchemy: The Magic of Original Thinking in a World of Mind-Numbing Conformity*

ABOUT THE AUTHOR

Registered Life Planner® and coach Justin King is one of the UK's most qualified independent financial advisers. Motivated by helping people find fulfilment, he supports others to take control of their lives and thrive in retirement. Justin is the co-author of *Ready, Steady, Retire! Plan Your Way to Success in a Redefined Retirement* and host of *The Retirement Café Podcast* and his YouTube channel, Justin_King.

Discover more at theretirementcafe.co.uk.

JUSTIN KING

The Retirement *Café* HANDBOOK

NINE ACCELERATORS *for a* SUCCESSFUL RETIREMENT

The Retirement Café®

Copyright © Justin King, 2023.

First published in Great Britain in 2023.

The Retirement Café®

Cover design by Design • Jessica

All rights reserved. No part of this work may be reproduced or utilised in any form by any means, electronic or mechanical, including photocopying, recording or by any information storage and retrieval system, without the prior written permission of the copyright holder.

While the author has made every effort to provide accurate telephone numbers, internet addresses, and other information at the time of publication, neither the publisher nor the author assumes any responsibility for errors or for changes that occur after publication. Further, the publisher does not have any control over and does not assume any responsibility for author or third-party websites or their content.

The interviews and conversations in this book are accurate to the best of the author's ability. All ideas expressed by the interviewees remain their intellectual property and are protected by copyright law. This book is for information and entertainment only. Nothing in this book constitutes financial advice. Please do not make any decisions based on its contents; seek professional independent financial advice first.

The moral right of the author has been asserted.

Paperback: 978-1-7394103-0-8
eBook: 978-1-7394103-1-5

To Kathy, thank you for your unwavering support and love.
Without you, this book would not have been possible.

To my amazing daughters, Olivia and Amy,
may you live your lives with kindness and curiosity.

To all my clients, thank you for trusting me.

Contents

1. What questions should you be asking? — 1
2. Where are you at, right now? — 5
3. What is a successful retirement? — 11
4. Levers and accelerators for a successful retirement — 15
5. Accelerator 1 – Redefining retirement — 21
6. Accelerator 2 – Having a purpose — 33
7. Accelerator 3 – It's never too late — 49
8. Accelerator 4 – The science of living better for longer — 61
9. Accelerator 5 – Taking control of your health and well-being — 73
10. Accelerator 6 – The Big D — 99
11. Accelerator 7 – Planning for a 30-year retirement — 123
12. Accelerator 8 – The role of investing — 155
13. Accelerator 9 – Care and the end of life — 179
14. What will you do now? — 199
15. Become the hero of your retirement story — 203

Resources for your retirement — *207*

Recommended reading — *211*

CHAPTER 1

What questions should you be asking?

What does it take to live a successful retirement?

According to the latest official figures, the number of UK adults aged 100 or older reached its highest ever level in 2020, rising to 15,210 – up almost a fifth from a year earlier. This significant increase in membership of the centenarian club was driven almost entirely by a surge in the number of 100 year olds living on the British Isles (up 52% from 4,980 in 2019 to 7,590 in 2020).

That's a lot of the oldest old in our society, and the numbers are forecast to continue rising. Even if you don't stick around long enough to get that all-important birthday card from His Majesty The King, your life expectancy today is much better than it was even a generation ago, which means more and more of us are living longer into our later lives.

But although we are likely to spend more time in retirement than ever before, so many of us are careering into this next stage of life uninformed and underprepared, living an existence far from what is deserved; a life of surviving when we could be thriving.

Despite the importance of getting retirement planning right, the average person on the street simply doesn't have access to this information or know the right questions to ask. It's not their fault; everything is stacked against them – we live in one of the most complex tax systems in the world. An attempt to 'simplify' pensions in 2006 did anything but. Add the care and welfare system and the rapidly evolving investment market to the mix, and you get one thing: complexity.

I have helped hundreds of people to cut through this complexity, allowing them to achieve fulfilling retirements through following my highly effective retirement planning framework, developed during my 30 years of experience as a financial planner. However, I realised there was a more significant challenge: a whole population of older people who need the insight that I was only delivering on a one-to-one basis.

So in 2017 I started hosting live events called The Retirement Café, which then spawned into a podcast. As well as imparting my own knowledge, I brought in subject matter experts to share their expertise with a wider audience. But while the events and podcast episodes delivered tremendous information, they left our attendees and listeners with unanswered questions and, in many cases, the information I shared provoked more questions than answers. I quickly came to realise that asking questions isn't the problem.

The problem is knowing which questions to ask. We don't know what we don't know. It's as simple as that.

In 2002, former US Secretary of Defense Donald Rumsfeld gave a news briefing about the lack of evidence linking the Iraqi government to the supply of weapons of mass destruction to terrorist groups. What could have otherwise been a relatively uneventful press conference made a lasting impression.

Rumsfeld explained: "There are known knowns; there are things we know we know. We also know there are known unknowns; that is to say, we know there are some things we do not know. But there are also unknown unknowns – the ones we don't know we don't know."

This category of unknown unknowns is always the hardest to deal with. How do we approach a subject as critical as retirement planning without knowing which questions to ask, because they fall within this definition of unknown unknowns?

In so many cases, I have seen clients and listeners bogged down in details around their pension pots' current and projected future value. Do I have enough money in my retirement pot? It's a question, but is it the right question?

As you approach this chapter in your own life, it's likely you'll have many questions yourself:

Will I outlive my money, or will my money outlive me?

How do I make the most of my wealth to last my lifetime and still leave a legacy for my family?

How can I make sure I continue to make sound financial decisions as I get older?

Will my spouse be looked after when I'm no longer here?

How do I talk to my family about inheritance?

This handbook will address all of these, but to ensure a successful experience, we must take a holistic approach and consider every aspect of retirement.

Since I started *The Retirement Café Podcast*, I've dedicated myself to seeking out and interviewing over 150 experts from all manner of fields, from finance to academia to health and wellness. The chapters ahead present a clear framework to follow, covering every area you need to live the best life possible in retirement. They have been carefully crafted, based on decades of experience and hundreds of meaningful conversations. You will hear from scientists, authors and those who are transforming our society for the better. I've also included conversations with people living with purpose in retirement, often in some unexpected ways.

Along with my listeners, I've learned a considerable amount. But condensing the most critical lessons from those conversations into one handy handbook? That's the mission I've tackled here.

This publication is the culmination of my learnings, my professional development and my experience advising hundreds of people entering and enjoying their retirement. I hope you have, in your hands right now, everything you need to know to ensure a successful retirement, which is exactly what I want for you.

This book has been designed as a working handbook, one you can dip in and out of throughout your retirement journey, a helpful companion for this next phase of your life. However, you'll get the most benefit if you read it all the way through initially so that you understand the framework as a whole and know all the elements to consider and plan for to ensure your wealth lasts a lifetime. And when specific challenges arise, you'll know where to come back to.

CHAPTER 2

Where are you at, right now?

Before you start making your plan for a successful retirement, it's helpful to know where you stand today.

In my experience, people in and approaching retirement usually find themselves on one of four levels:

Sadly, too many people are struggling in the lowest level of preparation. I call this the **overwhelmed zone**. People who find themselves here have certain common traits: they tend to be in denial about how much control they have over their health, for example, and they either believe there is nothing they can do to improve their declining health or that their current robust health will remain forever. Neither belief is accurate.

People in this zone also tend to feel helpless about their financial situation. They aren't sure how to make the best use of their limited or abundant resources to enjoy a wonderful retirement. Another common attribute I see, is people believing that life just happens to them. I'm sure you've met people who hold tight to this fatalistic attitude. Those with this mindset often lack the tools they need to take control at this unique stage of life to make it a positive and happy experience.

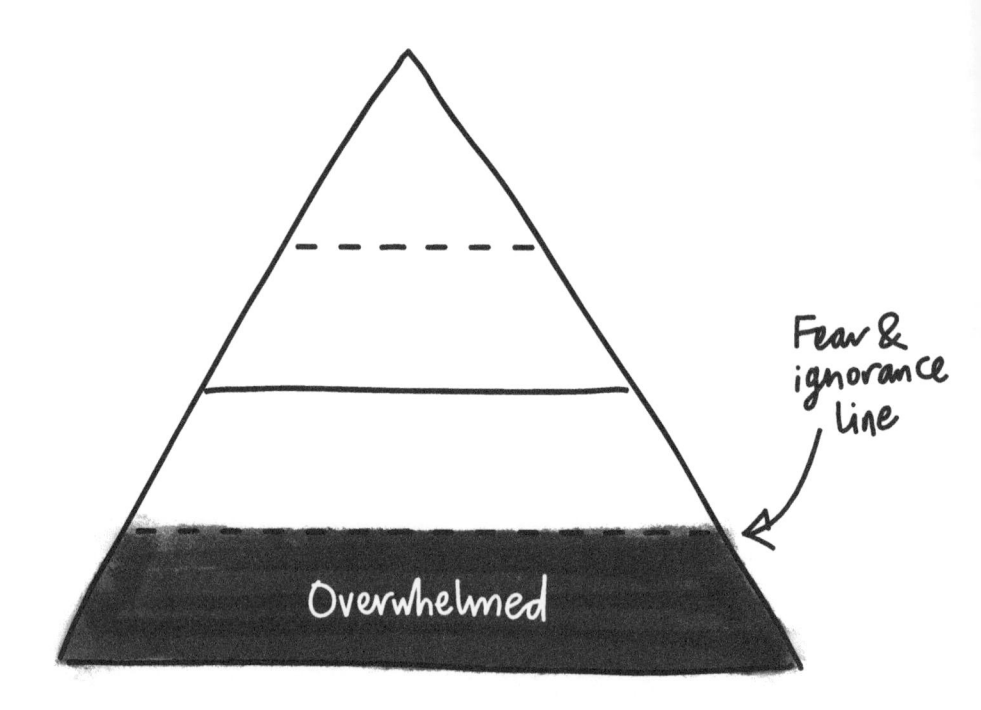

[Pyramid diagram: bottom shaded section labeled "Overwhelmed", with an arrow pointing to the dashed line above it labeled "Fear & ignorance line"]

People in this zone feel **overwhelmed** – and who can blame them? The thing is, being stuck at this level is not their fault. They're trapped behind what I call the 'Fear and Ignorance Line'. If that's you, you probably feel like the system is working against you. You might feel frozen and powerless to take constructive action, or that you have no control over your retirement.

Thankfully, this is a myth.

You can significantly change the quality of your life and the satisfaction you experience.

Taking small steps towards improving your retirement can make a substantial difference. In fact, you might even find you immediately leap up to the next level.

Chapter 2

Drifting

Overwhelmed

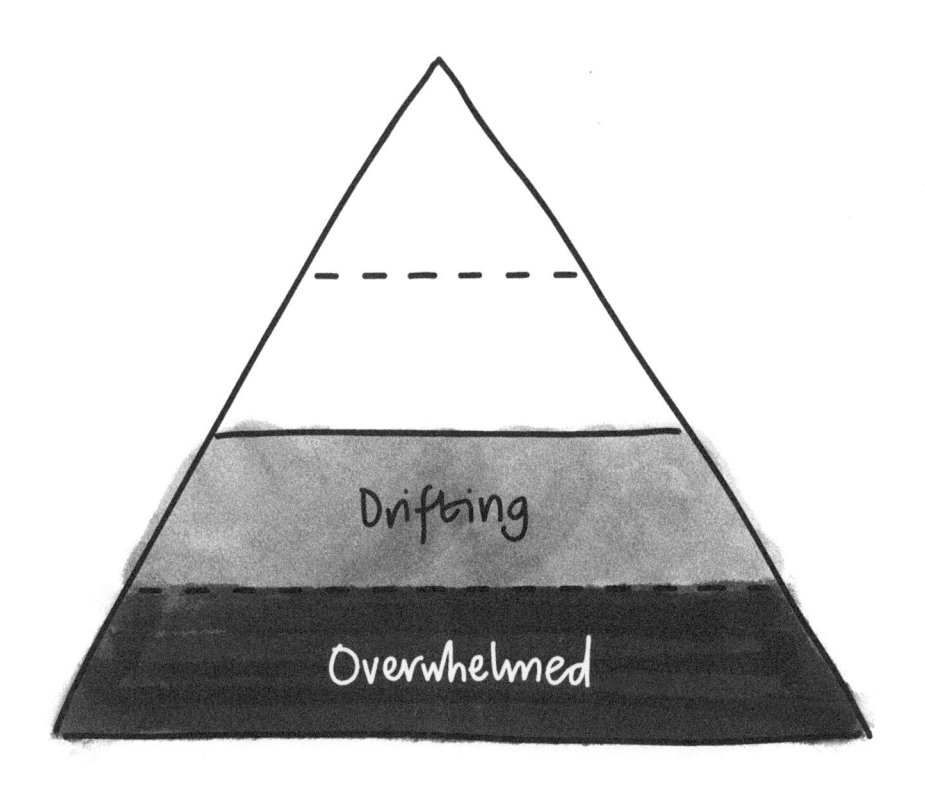

In this next zone, I find people are a little more optimistic about their health but still tend to rely too much on 'hopefully' being okay as they age. At the same time, members of this zone are doing what they believe is the right thing to make the best use of their money and resources to enjoy a good retirement.

If you're **drifting** at this level, you might feel like you're striving for a better, happier life. You're probably doing more of the things you want to do with your time and starting to be who you want to be. While you're in a better place than those in the overwhelmed zone, it can still feel like you're coasting into this next stage of life without any real purpose or direction. The key to moving upwards into a better place, is to engage with your retirement and really make the most of it.

In the next level up, I find people are keen to **participate** more in their retirement planning. If you're in this third zone, it's likely you're more engaged with your money, health and well-being. You've probably been proactive in making changes in your life and seen some improvements as a result. You will be actively planning for your future and putting your time, money and resources to good use.

Generally, I find that people here are pretty content with their lives. That's no bad thing. However, to continue moving up to reach the ideal place for your retirement, you need to take full ownership of your future.

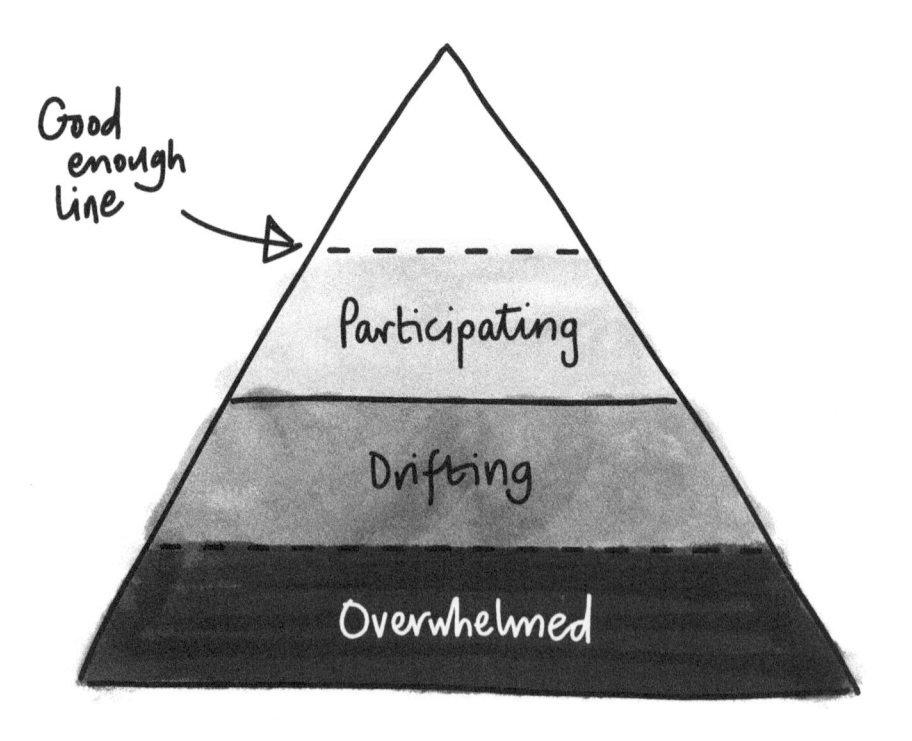

Good enough line → **Participating** / **Drifting** / **Overwhelmed**

The funny thing is, all too often, people get to this stage and bump up against what I call the 'Good Enough Line'. On the Good Enough Line, it's all too easy to buy into the myth that okay is good enough. Of course, 'good enough' traps you at that level when it is possible to achieve more. What if Steve Jobs had concluded that the iPod was good enough? Perhaps another tech firm would have developed the iPhone and iPad and become a trillion-dollar business instead. Think about it another way: what if you were buying a product or service, and the company selling to you said, "We're going to try and do a good enough job?" How would you feel?

Good enough isn't good enough, especially in your retirement. I want better for you. Once you realise that good enough has trapped you, you can consciously choose to continue climbing to the very top level of the pyramid.

Reaching the summit in the game of retirement is dramatically different. If you've made it to the top zone, you are trying to have the best possible health at all stages of your life. You have achieved financial freedom and have absolute choice about how you spend your time, money and resources. Most importantly, when you reach this level, you are genuinely **thriving** and making the most of this exceptional chapter of your life.

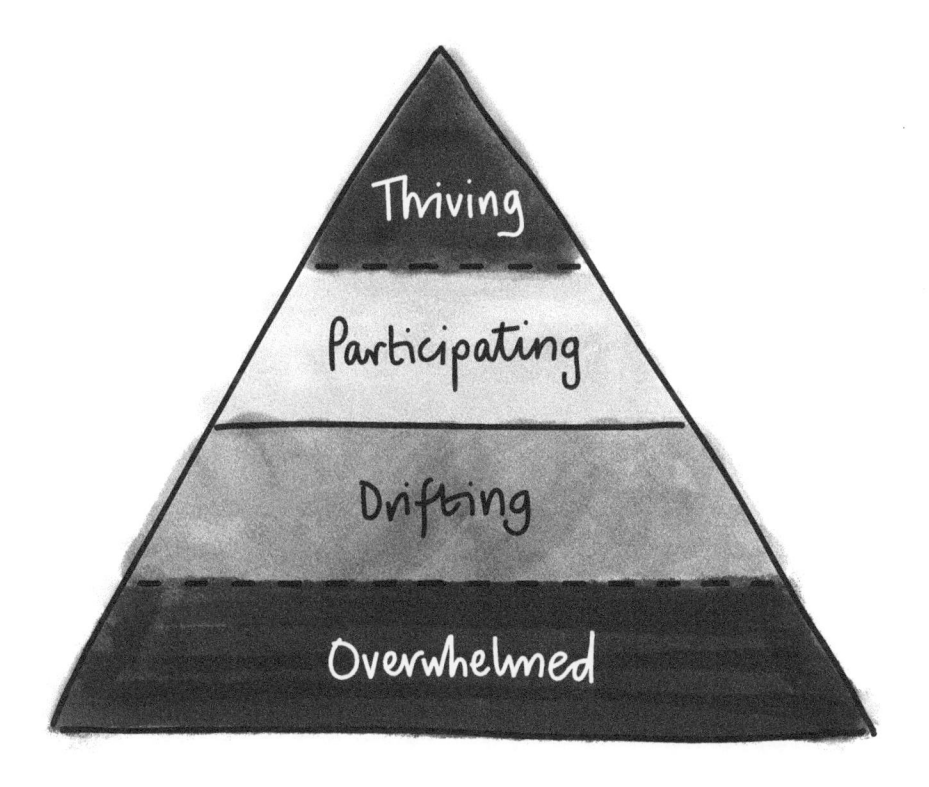

It takes commitment to get to the top zone and, equally, it takes commitment to stay there.

Looking at these four levels, give yourself an honest assessment: where do you feel you are right now? Where would you like to be? How are you positioned for your retirement?

My goal is to support you to reach the pinnacle of the pyramid and thrive in your retirement. As we move on to the next chapter, let's explore what that might look like.

CHAPTER 3

What is a successful retirement?

Frank, 62, came to me recently for a first meeting to help him work out how to turn his pension pot into a retirement income. Nine times out of ten, when a new client comes to my office, they ask me a question about their pension.

Or their investment portfolio. Or taxation.

Of course, these things are important, but they're not the secret to a successful retirement. When I asked Frank some deeper questions about what retirement looks like for him, he was bewildered. When I asked him to step back from the question of his pension and retirement income, he struggled to answer. Frank hadn't considered retirement beyond the value of his pension.

Frank isn't alone in this outlook. In fact, his reaction to my question is pretty common. Maybe you can even see a bit of yourself in Frank?

Based on my experience from chatting with dozens of experts on *The Retirement Café Podcast* and helping dozens more retire successfully, I've discovered something interesting: people tend to mainly focus on when they will have enough money to retire. I like to take a slightly different perspective and think of how we approach this stage of life as being like an iceberg.

Let me explain.

what you see above the water is only about 10% of the actual iceberg

wind direction

When can I afford to retire?

The true majesty of the iceberg is in its base

The iceberg will always move in the direction of its base

This focus on having enough money to fund retirement is similar to looking at the part of the iceberg that sits above the waterline. You don't need to have been a passenger on the RMS *Titanic* to know how much of the iceberg lies beneath the surface. You could visit a floating iceberg, take a photograph and maybe see a tenth of it – the true majesty of the iceberg is in its base. Regardless of how strong the wind is blowing, or in which direction, those gusts won't influence the iceberg's course – it will always move in the direction of its base, even if that is opposite to the direction of the wind.

And, bizarrely, that's also true in retirement.

Bear with me...

Any conversation about when you can afford to retire and how much you need to have saved is incredibly shallow. While important, it lacks the depth required to make meaningful decisions about your future. The most meaningful and vital conversation about retirement is understanding what is happening below the waterline. What does the real foundation look like at the base of your iceberg? Sitting immediately below the waterline is sometimes a less tangible part of the conversation about achieving the outcome you really want.

In my experience, what truly matters when it comes to your retirement are:

Vitality – are you in the best possible health, focused on continually improving your well-being to give yourself the best chance of living better, for longer?

Choice – do you understand how your time, money and resources become a source of freedom and independence, giving you the most choices in retirement?

Joy – are you making the most of this unique stage of life to do what you want to do and be who you want to be?

Think for a moment about those three questions. What would it mean for you if you had vitality in retirement, with the best possible chance of living better for longer? How would it feel to have more choices during your retirement, leading to deep joy from doing and being what matters most to you?

What would that feel like and look like?

If we think about vitality, choice and joy, as I hope you will as you read this book, we know just how critically important each is. Yet, as important as they are, a successful retirement isn't only about those three things. I believe it's about something more profound.

Take a second to imagine the moment you celebrate your 90th birthday. You're sitting in your rocking chair, looking back at 30 years of retirement and thinking, "Wow, wasn't that fantastic? Wasn't that the most amazing period of my life? I made a difference. I had great relationships with my family and friends. I was part of a community. I travelled. I learned new skills. I enjoyed spending time with my grandchildren." Whatever your reflection at that age might be, these are typically the achievements people want to enjoy at this stage of their life. More than vitality, choice and joy, I believe you deserve a deeply satisfying and fulfilling retirement – one without regrets. Isn't that what you truly want?

When can I afford to retire?

- Vitality
- Choice
- Joy

I BELIEVE you DESERVE a truly fulfilling retirement

With this insight, I decided to develop a practical, logical how-to framework explaining how to have a truly fulfilling retirement so that you can reach the level of majesty at the bottom of your iceberg.

Let's take a look…

CHAPTER 4

Levers and accelerators for a successful retirement

When I set out to write this book, my goal was to ensure you have everything you need to know for a successful, fulfilling retirement. I know that achieving this goal results from three things: vitality, choice and joy – **vitality** to live a healthy life, both physically and mentally, for as long as possible, **choice** and the financial freedom to do the things you want to do, and **joy** that comes from living a life that brings you happiness and contentment.

Vitality, choice and joy.

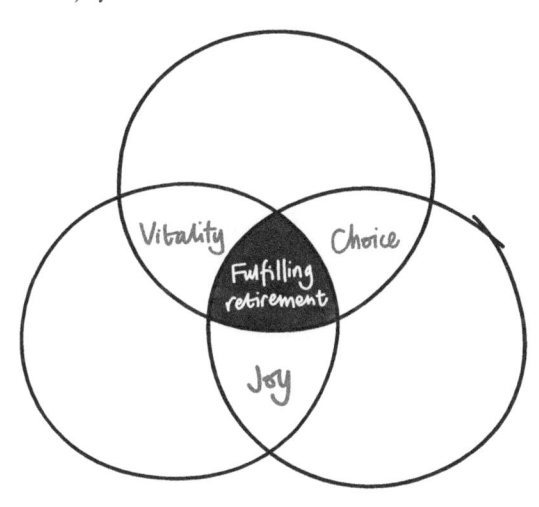

Are any of those three outcomes important to you?

Most of the conversations I have tell me that all three factors are important for a successful retirement, and I agree!

The big question then is, how do we get all three outcomes? What levers drive vitality, choice and joy? In other words, what do you need to have in place to achieve vitality, choice and joy? In my experience, the lever that has the most significant impact on vitality and choice is the **purpose** lever.

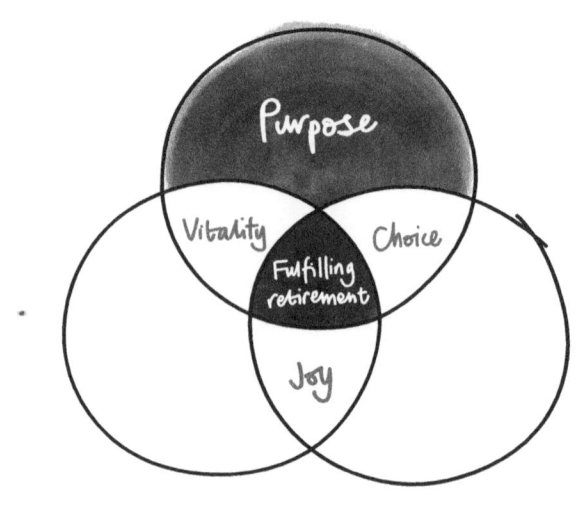

All the conversations I have had on this topic illustrate the importance of having a clear direction for your retirement. Creating meaning for this stage in life is your opportunity to move from drifting through your retirement years to genuinely flourishing.

What do you want the next 30 years of your life to look like?

The lever critical to driving vitality and joy is **self-care** – looking after your physical and emotional well-being. Self-care is all about taking action to be in the best possible health while making the most of those opportunities that become available to you. The self-care lever moves you from being ambivalent to being fully engaged in your health and well-being.

Would you agree that if you have purpose in life and look after yourself, you will have vitality?

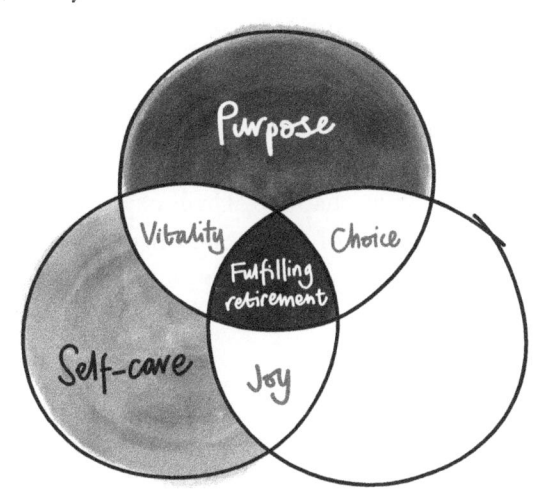

The third lever drives choice and joy, and it's called **planning**. Planning is all about moving from taking a somewhat accidental approach to the next chapter of your life, to being more deliberate and creating plans that support and enable the retirement you want to live. Does it make sense that you will make the most of your choices if you have purpose and a clear plan for your retirement?

If you deliberately plan with the intention of a fulfilling retirement and know that you're engaged in looking after yourself, isn't this likely to bring joy?

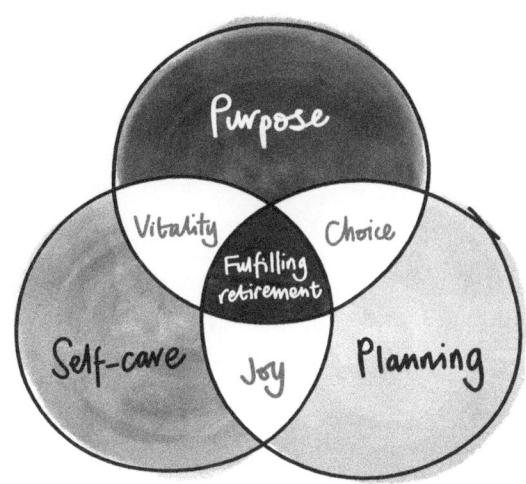

The alternative to engaging these three levers is to live through your retirement years with no direction. If you don't look after yourself, you will have no confidence in your future. If you don't have a plan, you will have no framework to enable you to live the retirement you want.

In my framework for a successful and fulfilling retirement, I apply nine key accelerators to drive these three levers – three accelerators for each lever. In the following chapters, I will explore each of these nine accelerators in detail, drawing on expert insights from my podcast guests and arming you with the tools you need to pull all three levers and deliver a fulfilling retirement.

The nine accelerators are:

1. **Redefining retirement:** clarifying what retirement means to you and challenging stereotypes of what this time should look like.

2. **Having a purpose:** understanding how to bring meaning to your retirement.

3. **It's never too late:** exploring opportunities to fulfil your dreams and ambitions.

4. **The science of living better for longer:** understanding the research behind ageing and living well in retirement.

5. **Taking control of your health and well-being:** learning how to look after your physical and mental health during your retirement.

6. **The Big D:** understanding, living with and preventing dementia.

7. **Planning for a 30-year retirement:** creating a financial plan for an abundant retirement.

8. **The role of investing:** understanding the reasons to invest and what makes a successful investment strategy.

9. **Care and the end of life:** preparing a plan for when you need care and your final stage of life.

Most people have mastered some of these accelerators but very few achieve all nine, which means too many people are missing out on the coveted 'sweet spot' at the heart of the framework – living their ideal retirement.

I don't want that for you.

As you look at these nine accelerators driving three levers and consider your answers to the questions I ask throughout the book, you might feel woefully unprepared for your retirement. That's not unusual; it's how many of my clients feel at this stage of their journey. And it's exactly why I wrote this book – so you don't have to navigate this path alone. I'm here to guide you every step of the way.

Let's do this.

CHAPTER 5

Accelerator 1 – Redefining retirement

Let me ask you a question:

How clear are you about what retirement looks like to you?

Where would you position yourself on a scale of 1 to 10, where 1 is *'I've given it some thought'* and 10 is *'I have a crystal clear view of what my retirement will look like'*?

The thing is, retirement has changed. It's no longer what it used to be. Improved and improving longevity is changing the nature of retirement. Sir Muir Gray, who we'll meet in Chapter 8, redefines it as a 'renaissance'. Your renaissance presents an opportunity to remap this later stage of life so you can build the life you truly want in terms of how you live, work and experience your relationships with others.

Take a moment to picture your retirement. Many people will tell you it consists of golf, cruises and spending precious time with family or in the garden, that it's time to reap the rewards of all those years of hard work, shifting the emphasis from work to leisure.

What do you think retirement is about?

On *The Retirement Café Podcast*, I recently spoke with Laura Page, a photographer and social activist who is challenging our preconceptions about retirement. Looking through the images on her website, www.laurapage.co.uk, you might not immediately believe these are pictures of modern retirement: a world-champion weightlifter, a dancer and a craftsman, all in their 70s, 80s or older. They don't meet our typical expectations of what someone in their retirement years might be doing or might look like.

Everyone's experience of retirement is unique.

The first accelerator for the purpose lever is **redefining retirement**. When we consider redefining retirement, I want to challenge your perceptions about ageing. This chapter explores what retirement could mean and look like, helping you understand the opportunities available to you today.

By creating your unique version of retirement, you can truly flourish.

Living in an age of longevity

One of my podcast guests, Andrew J Scott, is Professor of Economics at London Business School and has been an academic his entire working life. He offers an insightful look at the bigger picture and helps answer the question: how is our increasing longevity changing our lives in retirement?

Co-author of *The 100-Year Life: Living and Working in an Age of Longevity*, Professor Scott agrees that the increasing length of our lives on Planet Earth is having a profound impact on retirement. Life expectancy improvement is often called one of the great achievements of the 20th century, but Professor Scott doesn't think we've yet seized the key opportunities this longer life has to offer.

The story says there are now more older people and they are (typically) not productive: "Old people get ill and become a burden on society." And that's going to be a significant problem for the future. However, as

Chapter 5

Professor Scott explains, this narrative is a negative one, a 'spreadsheet' mentality applied to a social issue that is both a challenge and an opportunity.

As we've seen, based on key statistics and on average, we're living longer, with the fastest growing demographic group being those aged 100 and over. Not only are we welcoming more centenarians, but we're staying healthier for longer, which is brilliant news.

In the 20th century, one of the key financial issues was life insurance: making sure your families and loved ones were looked after. However, due to our lengthening lifespans, the big issue is becoming longevity insurance.

Will you outlive your assets? As a retirement planner, I devote a great deal of my time to understanding whether my clients' money can outlast their life expectancies. Longevity insurance is also concerned with whether you will outlive your relationships and sense of purpose. As ever, financial planning is as much about life as it is about money!

So, how can you ensure this doesn't happen to you?

One suggestion offered by Professor Scott is to look after your diet. But living well in retirement is about more than the physical aspects – it's about how engaged you are with life and understanding that age is malleable.

Professor Scott tells me we need to free our minds and recognise that the way we think can influence how we age – that's why we are remaining healthier for longer and living for longer. He says our future is about more than financial aspects and we need to work hard to try and improve that future. That 'mindset malleability' needs a very different approach because we have to start thinking more about our future – after all, we will have more future than ever before to think about!

Most governments say age 65-plus is 'old'. But that's no longer the case because, first of all, people are ageing better – 70 is the new 65. Secondly, diversity is central to understanding what's happening in this new age of longevity. People age very differently. We have these out-of-date stereotypes about ageing, even on an individual level. We look back at what our grandparents did, or at our parents, and say, "That's what it is to be old." But ageing is being redefined. Look at The Rolling Stones – Jagger and his bandmates are still touring in 2023, more than five decades into their career.

I agree with Professor Scott when he says we need to think about our stereotypes a little differently. For example, with the use of technology and advanced robotics used in manufacturing, new approaches could potentially elongate your career. With the physical aspects of work supported by new technology, the natural results of ageing will no longer force retirement.

Reinventing your identity

If you're thinking about retirement in the near future, Professor Scott says you need to start thinking about how you can change and reinvent your identity, like a teenager searching for their place in the world. He believes the ability to adapt and deal with transitions is incredibly important as we get older. As machines become more machine-like, we'll see humans needing to become more human-like and the most important jobs will be where human skills come to the fore. All of this change could even benefit older people.

Evidence suggests that, over time, your brain shifts what it's best at. Empathy, leadership, bringing teams together – all these skills tend to improve as we get older. This is important to remember in the shifting employment landscape.

Professor Scott warns us that the old ways of being employed until age 60 or 65 are no longer working so well. We know, for example, that pension pots are struggling to cope because retirement is getting longer. Traditional employment is struggling with improved longevity too. How can we, as individuals, keep up with the skills required in a rapidly changing world?

Longevity of life is changing our social norms and, as already mentioned, we need to change our mindsets to go along with the changes. As a teenager, it's easy to create the life you'd like. But as you grow older and

Chapter 5

technology changes, you have no idea how to live your life by the right design. As I mentioned, we naturally copy what has happened before, but with these deep-seated changes on the horizon, we need a different approach.

Professor Scott says we need to take responsibility and, because you will have more future, you need to invest more in it, whether you're 20 or 50, or even 90 years old.

How do you invest your time?

When I interviewed Professor Scott, we were in the middle of the Covid-19 pandemic and working life as we knew it was changing, with more people working from home. Our work environments became less important for forming relationships, as the new default environment for relationships became our internal households and local communities. In our new system, 'work' took on a new concept which, for many, has continued even after the pandemic. 'Work' in the 20th century was the time you were paid for by your employer. But actually, there's a whole bunch of leisure activities that can also be considered work and these activities are things you do that pay a return later in life, such as relationships, your health and your skills, thinking consciously about leisure, spending time with your children and nurturing your relationship with them. It's a shift in awareness and understanding that, right now, the best investment of your time isn't necessarily just 'working'.

Would your 90-year-old self be thankful to your 50-year-old self for the decisions you made? What you do in your 50s will influence what you do in your 60s, which will influence what you do in your 70s. The skill that has become more important is being able to relate to your future self because you've got more future selves, and working on that way of thinking is incredibly important.

Most people assume that living longer is about more years, but it's actually not – it really concerns this period from age 50 to 70, a new 'late middle age' that's emerged. It can be a great opportunity, but it does require work. The good news is, no matter what age you are – 50, 60, 70, 80, or even 90 – if you do something now, you can affect the future.

Of course, the earlier you start, the better. Working on trying to be kind to your future self is an important life skill.

How to cope with longevity

Professor Scott suggests three ways to approach the challenges and opportunities that stem from improved longevity:

Explore – there are no simple answers. You have to go out, be open-minded and investigate change. Once you see what's out there, it's about having the confidence to start making changes.

Narrate – this is an accumulation of things based around two aspects: one is rethinking your concept of age and what you do because you have more of a future. You must invest in your future self more and do things differently.

The second is recognising that this is your story to paint and it's likely to have more stages and transitions. Try to put yourself in situations where you're going to grow and change. Be comfortable with no longer being that person who knows who they are.

Relate – we know from all the life studies that money makes you happier; it just doesn't make you happy. The most important things in life are relationships. However, if you are changing what you do and going through these life transitions, what are the relationships you need to focus on, and how do you work on them?

This three-pronged approach can help you curate a retirement that suits you and fits your changing needs as you get older – after all, your age shouldn't be what defines you.

What would Muffy do?

When you were in your mid-30s, did the prospect of growing old scare you? It did for Dominique Afacan and Helen Cathcart. To them, old age was an unhappy place, mostly filled with loneliness, rocking chairs and

Chapter 5

possibly some tea and biscuits – if they were lucky! Their worries about what their futures held were astounding: everything felt bleak.

Dominique and Helen decided they should do something about this fear, so they created Bolder, a book and a website on a mission to change perceptions about growing older. They met and interviewed a selection of people who they would have typically dumped into a homogenous category of 'old'. They thought, "Let's see what they have to say; either they'll change our perceptions of what it means to grow older, or we'll at least hear some hard-earned wisdom in the process."

Here are two inspiring stories from the many people they interviewed:

Pierre Gruneberg, 87 years old at the time of interview, is the oldest swimming instructor in France. Pierre has been giving swimming lessons at the Four Seasons Cap-Ferrat for most of his life. He is so energetic and full of zest; every morning before work, he swims a mile to a lighthouse in the Mediterranean Sea!

Muffy, also 87 years old at the time of interview, has a fantastic attitude about life and plays tennis frequently. Muffy has witnessed a certain amount of tragedy in her life, but as she says, "I am inspired by tennis; you win some, you lose some, and you fight again." Whenever Dominique or Helen feel slightly negative, they ask, "What would Muffy do?"

Both women soon realised the stereotypes they were previously tuning into were completely inaccurate in most cases. So many people they met were marrying in their 80s, finding love much later on in life, beginning new careers, being physically active and not dressing in the way they associated with older people. They realised that everyone they met looked after themselves and kept themselves active with an exercise regime, be that something like playing tennis, or simply balancing on one leg while cleaning their teeth! Dominique and Helen are now really excited about growing older and hope to be as active, relevant and tuned into society as they are now.

Should perceptions of the older generations change? I believe they should. However, there does seem to be a conspiracy of silence surrounding retirement.

Everybody who experiences retirement says how wonderful it is. But are they being honest with you? Genuinely honest about that first taste of retirement? When you lose all your colleagues alongside leaving your job, you also lose your fulfilling role and a great deal of intellectual stimulation. It's not always easy.

One of my podcast guests, Maggy Pigott, author of *How to Age Joyfully: Eight Steps to a Happier, Fuller Life*, says you might compare retirement with having a baby. Everyone tells expectant mothers how wonderful it will be, but when you have that new baby in your arms and you speak to another parent, you will be trading tales about sleepless nights – you feel like you might never sleep for a whole night again! And this is precisely how some may feel when they retire! It's an adjustment. Once that adjustment is made, you'll wake up one morning and think, "I've got 30 years hopefully ahead of me – what am I going to do with them?" This adjustment brings a time of freedom and gives you more control over your life. Having retired from a distinguished 37-year career in the legal profession, Maggy believes retirement is a time for making new friends, looking around and seeing where you want to go and what new things you might want to do.

As David Bowie once said, "Ageing is that extraordinary process whereby you become the person you always should have been."

But is it always that straightforward? Many people aren't able to choose their time of transition, but instead are forced into making life changes earlier than planned. Losing your job makes you dig deep and find those hidden talents you didn't realise you had. Tim Drake, the author of *Generation Cherry*, had to do this in his 50s. The recession hit, he lost his company and he had to build everything up from scratch. However, he now thinks this was the best thing to ever happen to him. Finding these long-forgotten talents helped Tim to feel so much better about himself when adjusting to his new life. He realised he had so much more to give.

Tim is now 75 and extremely happy. He does a mixture of charity work, money-earning projects and creating. He is always busy but never stressed. The concept of Tim's book is that his generation, dubbed 'Generation Cherry', had a cherry on everything: there were plenty of jobs that came with great pensions and working life was set up for them. However, the cherry shrivels with time and Tim's generation must adapt, as we've already heard from Professor Scott.

But with adaptation comes unforeseen joy.

Tim believes that once retired, if you stay engaged in work of some kind, even if it's half a day a week, you're still in touch with the working world and all that goes with it. If your children are talking to you about work and money, you know what they're talking about; you won't feel like a spectator knowing nothing.

Everyone, no matter their age, has unreleased potential.

Reimagining where you live

In the 1980s, the norm for growing old was staying in your home for as long as possible until you had a crisis. Once the crisis hit, you were then moved to a care home or a geriatric ward, which, if you ever saw one, was not a place you or your family ever wanted to be! Things started to change slowly: specialist housing and a range of services and supportive care were brought in, which meant people could stay in their homes for much longer.

When I spoke to Jamie Bunce from Inspired Villages and Nick Sanderson from Audley Villages – two of the leading Integrated Retirement Community operators – they reminded me there are currently 12 million people aged 65 and over in the UK. That figure is due to rise to 18 million by 2030–2035. The number of people over 85 will double in this time too. Currently, there are only approximately 80,000 properties in housing facilities or complexes where care can be provided on site. Sadly, the supply-and-demand ratio is out of proportion, and your choice of where to live if you need support is very narrow as you grow older.

Is it time to tear up the rulebook? What kind of home do you want? Where would you like to live when you're older? What would you like to experience? What pressure would you like to have taken away from you without your independence being taken too?

During the Covid-19 pandemic, many retired people felt isolated and alone during the lockdown and isolation periods. This was exacerbated by our traditional community structure changing – high street shops are closing due to new shopping habits, and the hearts of our communities are being ripped out as many people who live in quaint villages in the country rise early to commute to work.

To address these challenges, positive change is starting to happen – Integrated Retirement Communities are being built for the older generations.

Does this idea fill you with dread? Does it bring to mind images of stuffy apartments with people telling you what to do and taking away your independence?

Maybe it's time to take another look at what's really happening.

In these new village communities, you can pop into the café for a quiet cup of coffee but still be surrounded by peers, attend events and dinners, collect your newspapers from the shop and read them on the bench, all while living in high-quality housing. Each community tends to have a mix of independent and assisted living, centred around holistic well-being; the physical, mental, social and financial well-being of the people who live there is a priority, along with that of their families and colleagues.

Deciding where to live is one way of redefining your retirement. Moving to a community like this, with restaurants, cafés, bars, swimming pools, saunas, steam rooms, fitness studios, craft rooms and gardens could enable you to live a full life without relying on family and loved ones. As you grow older, your needs will change, and those changing needs are bound to be individual. Traditionally, living options for older people were very binary in terms of matching people's needs with the support available. They didn't offer the flexibility found in these new retirement villages where, as your needs change, support is already in place for you on site.

Could moving to a community like this be on your agenda? If it is, make sure you are fully aware of all the cost implications and what care and support is available as you get older.

Renting vs buying

Have you ever thought about renting in retirement? As people get older, their priorities and viewpoints often change when it comes to housing options. Renting can offer the opportunity to release capital so you can invest in enjoying and exploring other things in life.

If you decide buying is the option for you, bear in mind that when people sell their family house of 25 or 30 years, 80% of the proceeds, on average, are used to buy their next property. This means equity is released, which can be used for day-to-day living so you can do more of the things you want to do and live the way you want to. Perhaps this means travelling, saying yes to more exciting pursuits or being able to support loved ones who need a helping hand.

Senior living can, and should be, the best years of your life. Why shouldn't it? You've probably cleared all your debts, your obligations have been met, you know what your income is, you know what capital you've got. Enjoy it! Make the most of it!

How do you redefine your retirement?

We're in the middle of a retirement revolution and more and more people are challenging the status quo on stereotypical assumptions about what it means to be retired. From housing innovations to intergenerational technology, there are more options than ever to help you live a retirement that suits you and harness greater opportunities without being defined by out-of-date notions of what this time of your life should look like.

Key takeaways

- To thrive in not only a changing time of your life but an ever-changing world, adaptability is key. Don't be afraid to reinvent yourself and embrace your evolving skill sets.

- Follow the three steps to coping with longevity: explore (seek out solutions and be open to new opportunities),

> narrate (write your own story but accept there will be growth and change along the way) and relate (invest time in your relationships; they're the most important thing in life).
>
> - Fostering a positive mindset towards ageing is essential to a happy retirement and will not only lead to a more fulfilling experience, but you could live longer too!

So what do you say? Are you ready to join the revolution?

Let's return to the question I asked you at the beginning of the chapter:

How clear are you about what retirement looks like to you?

Where would you position yourself on a scale of 1 to 10, where 1 is *'I've given it some thought'* and 10 is *'I have a crystal clear view of what my retirement will look like'*?

One of the tools I use with clients to help them answer this question is called 'Ideal Day, Ideal Week and Ideal Year'. It allows people to consider and design a day, a week, a year and, ultimately, a life that reflects the retirement they want.

Consider what you want your life to be like in each decade of your retirement. Your vitality, attitude and needs will change as you grow older, so consider how this will impact your life.

- Do you want to travel?

- Are you living in the right property for the rest of your life? Will you want or need to move at some point?

- Who do you want to spend more, or less, time with?

This exercise is a good starting point for designing your retirement.

CHAPTER 6

Accelerator 2 – Having a purpose

I believe everyone has a purpose in life – maybe you just haven't found yours yet?

As we toil away in the hustle and bustle of our everyday lives, it's effortless to neglect pondering our purpose. We're swamped. So busy, in fact, we often fail to pause and ask the right questions – the crucial questions that make the difference between having a clear purpose and direction, or drifting along until the end.

I get it: work, life and family take up so much of our time. The obstacles present themselves with frightening regularity. We tell ourselves we can't plan for our future because we've got children. We can't make plans for later because of the size of our mortgage. We can't work out what's important to us because we're too busy. And, because of these obstacles, we don't make deliberate progress in life.

What I've learned from my experience working with hundreds of clients over the years is that there is another way. We can redefine our lives and clearly define our purpose – at any stage of life.

This is the basis of the second accelerator for the purpose lever: **having a purpose.**

I'm not for one moment claiming this is easy. It isn't. Most people don't take decisive action in their lives, because they're terrified of what that involves.

Sure, there are financial implications. Making big changes in your life often means putting everything on the line. You could be moving from a known, safe environment to one that is uncertain and perceived to be risky, or moving from the knowledge of a regular pay cheque to an environment where you don't know where your next income is coming from – that's frightening.

In fact, it's a big flipping leap!

I know for sure that the process of financial planning can secure the money side of things, and doing so opens up a whole world of possibilities. With the money worries taken care of, you can explore options and possibilities that were previously off limits to you. You can, within reason, do more or less what you like. Your biggest challenge then becomes choosing from all the options laid out in front of you.

I recently met with a couple for the first time. One of them has cancer and the prognosis isn't good. If he's lucky, he has a year left to live.

Their solicitor recommended they talk to me and they arrived fully equipped with their numbers. I listened and eventually asked if we could take a step back: what was the ultimate goal of working with me? What would a wonderful outcome look like? What one or two lines would you attach to having a relationship with me as your financial planner?

The answer was clear: they wanted to make sure that when he dies, she has got someone around the corner she can trust to help her make great decisions. He wants peace of mind that his wife will have wise counsel.

I ask my clients a lot of questions, but one I like to go back to on a regular basis is one I've borrowed from George Kinder (more about him and financial life planning later): if tonight is your last night on Earth, what will you yearn for as you turn out the light?

The aim of this question is to encourage you to think about the things you haven't been able to do yet. All the things you wanted to do in life but haven't yet fit in during your relatively short time on the planet. It's also thinking about who you wanted to be but haven't yet had the chance. Did you always want to be a nurse, but the opportunity never seemed to arrive? Or to foster children? Or to feel less anxious?

Few of us know how long we've got left. We all know our date of birth, but relatively few people know with any certainty their date of death. If you've got a terminal illness, you probably have more clarity around your regrets and the things you want to achieve in life. If you're approaching retirement, say in your late 50s or early 60s, it can be much harder to step back and ask yourself that question. Perhaps the impetus is missing. But when I'm chatting with the chap who will die within the next 12 months, the motivation to reflect is clearly there.

The important questions I ask my clients, and I would encourage you to ask yourself (and for your partner to ask themself too), are:

- What would you change about your life if money was no object?

- What would you change about your life if you knew you had just five more years to live?

- If your life were to end tomorrow, in what way would your life have been incomplete?

I've adapted these questions from 'The Three Questions' developed by George Kinder and Kinder Institute of Life Planning, which are used as part of a programme of trainings that lead to the Registered Life Planner® designation.

Take time, alone, to ponder your answers, then write them down. Answer the questions in order. Try not to dwell on the questions too much; it's best to write the first things that pop into your mind, but then consider whether there's anything else you want to add.

It's important to complete this exercise independently from your partner, and having someone who's not close to you to help facilitate a discussion between you both about your answers will achieve the best outcome.

The purpose of these questions is to help you clarify and prioritise what's most important to you, and the answers should form the foundation of your retirement plan. It's the starting point and can help you uncover – or reaffirm – your purpose so that you can then set about making these important things happen.

The path you choose to achieve your goals in life might not always be the most obvious but there's more than one way to achieve your desired outcome. Having a clear objective about what you would like to achieve in life and the person you want to be doesn't necessarily lead to clarity around the steps to take to get there. But without that clarity of a goal, it's almost impossible to take any steps in the right direction, unless you are fortunate enough to stumble there by accident.

When you pursue something new, it helps to have purpose. We're living in an age when anyone can be anything. You can radically transform your identity to achieve almost anything you want, at any stage in life. We face infinite choices, which means we must narrow those down based on our chosen purpose. You might eliminate some choices based on the stuff you don't enjoy doing. That's fine.

But once you establish your priorities, you achieve the sort of clarity that can lead to incredible outcomes.

So what would bring meaning to your retirement?

One of the foundations of a successful retirement is having a clear purpose; being part of something bigger than yourself that gets you out of bed in the morning, day after day. As we live longer, with hopefully many more healthy years ahead, this sense of purpose becomes even more important.

As we explore the 'having a purpose' accelerator, I'll share why it's so important and, critically, how to identify what will bring meaning to your retirement, bringing in perspectives and expertise from a number of podcast guests. Knowing your purpose will allow you to live your future years with intention and deep satisfaction.

Finding freedom

There's a movement happening within the financial planning profession that places a focus on life rather than money.

Spearheading this exciting shift is my friend George Kinder. He's a mentor and teacher and has been very influential in both my career and personal life. Through his books, workshops and public speaking engagements, George has trained thousands of financial professionals globally (including me!) in financial life planning.

This is the approach I discussed in the introduction to this chapter and one I adopted many years ago in my retirement planning business: helping clients identify what's truly important to them, what they haven't yet had the chance to do, who they haven't yet had the chance to be and making sure this forms the basis of their financial plan for retirement.

My conversation with George for *The Retirement Café Podcast* drove home his core objective: to bring greater levels of freedom everywhere. And we all want freedom, don't we?

Plenty of the soon-to-be retirees I talk with are planning to achieve financial freedom and they also want to give back. You may be able to relate. Perhaps you also have a feeling you want to contribute during this phase of your life. After all, you have a lot to contribute. You have wisdom accumulated over 50 or 60 years and will soon be freed from the constraints of earning a living because you've saved well enough to look after yourself so you don't have to go to work. Financial freedom brings with it the freedom to explore and contribute in other ways.

It's time to look for that more significant purpose: what will bring meaning to your life?

This requires some deep thought.

One of the other things George touches on in his latest book, *A Golden Civilization & The Map of Mindfulness*, is something I'm also very passionate about: entrepreneurial spirit. This is not just about the entrepreneurial spirit in the classic 'I'm a shopkeeper or a self-employed person just starting a business' kind of way. This is the entrepreneurial spirit within you. George feels everyone has some entrepreneurial spirit within them.

I think that when retirees get to that position in life where they've suddenly got a bit more time, they're not responsible for children (although they tell me that never finishes!) on a day-to-day basis and they're also not responsible for going to work, it's time to find their entrepreneurial spirit. Asking the right questions, having an empathic ear and having time to explore what your entrepreneurial spirit could be, may just result in it being revealed.

George believes we would be kinder if we were all living purposeful, fulfilling lives: we would be more generous, and there would be more community and caring. I certainly cannot argue with that. If everyone was living those kinds of lives, a natural effect would be less conflict, less anger and possibly less ego (ego in the negative sense rather than the positive).

And what better place to start than with yourself as you approach retirement!

Life beyond work

Another podcast guest, Celia Dodd, told me about her research for her book on retirement, *Not Fade Away: How to Thrive in Retirement*. A journalist and feature writer for national newspapers, Celia started to have conversations with people about what to expect from this next stage of life. By talking to more than 60 retired people from all walks of life, as well as experts in the field, she found that although retirement can be a hugely positive experience for some, for others it can also be a significant challenge.

Celia realised a lot of people don't feel very happy at this stage in their lives. A survey by Ipsos in conjunction with the Centre for Ageing Better found that Britons are overwhelmingly negative about old age. Only 30% agree they are looking forward to old age, while more than double (68%) disagree with this statement.

But why?

Celia believes a lot of people don't want to retire. While some want to stop work, many would prefer to combine some part-time work with volunteering and hobbies. And while it's wonderful we have so much choice about how to spend our time, these options result in some tough decisions, which can become quite overwhelming. These expectations can continue to weigh heavily on us in retirement. In Celia's experience, everyone manages that weight of expectation differently because, of course, everyone is different.

She found that finding purpose is the big challenge for most people and requires a level of soul-searching. But maybe it's not found by sitting, staring deep into space. Maybe purpose is best discovered by talking with other people and exploring ideas together, which is what I aim to help people do by asking those important financial life planning questions.

Trial and error

Celia believes you need to try all kinds of different work, volunteering and hobbies to discover what suits you. Sometimes it's a case of trial and error.

In her book, Celia recalls a retired policeman, who travelled to Nepal to volunteer following an earthquake. Unfortunately, while he was there he had an accident and had to return home. However, he was determined to try again and returned to Nepal where, this time, he found a different style of volunteering that suited him far better.

Another woman Celia spoke to moved to a different part of the country when she retired. It was a disaster – she became depressed and found the lack of social contact difficult to deal with. Eventually, she decided to move into a co-housing project, where she is now much happier.

Building a bridge

I recall Celia sharing her dad's experience of a sad retirement. He struggled when he gave up work and became very depressed. Celia told me that he never fully recovered. I come across people like that regularly: people who can't cope without the status afforded to them by their work, or without the social networks created by employment. Their purpose has faded away and they haven't managed to discover a new purpose.

But this isn't the case for every retiree. Celia tells me a story that shatters this stereotype of the man with the high-status job who doesn't find retirement easy. She came across plenty of these walking, talking 'stereotypes' who were, instead, genuinely enjoying their life in retirement. She mentions a former television producer who would work 14-hour days, sometimes even longer. When they spoke, he was loving retirement and just enjoying the simple pleasures of life, like being able to walk up and down the beach, experience delicious food and see friends.

When Celia reflects on her dad's experience, she emphasises that he hadn't thought about the future. He hadn't planned what the next phase might look like, because work was the be-all and end-all to him. What Celia's father didn't have were robust social networks outside of work. She advises anyone approaching retirement to take note of recent research showing the importance of putting strong networks in place before you retire – they serve as a bridge between your old life and your new life. Your social networks can be based around the things you already love doing. Perhaps that's your walking group or book club. Build that bridge!

Finding purpose as a couple

Home life can also be an adjustment: the transition out of work is a fundamental lifestyle change and maybe the children are leaving home too. These changes can impact couples' relationships as well. If you've both enjoyed careers, or perhaps one of you has been raising the children, then all of a sudden, your previous roles have evaporated. Neither of you has those responsibilities any more. It's inevitable that your relationship will shift. Celia explains that to see these changes positively, you can view retirement as the shake-up that many couples need on occasion. This demands that you almost reinvent your relationship, or at least think hard about it. She believes the best way to do that is by talking to each other, and asking and answering those important life planning questions, together as a couple.

Studies show that the transitional period can be quite difficult for couples but after that, retirement can really improve marriage. Of course, part of the transition is that 'territory thing' – whoever has been at home has to adjust to having another person there in the house. You've got to work out your territory.

Celia tells me about a former teacher who was worried because he likes listening to music throughout the day but his wife doesn't. They didn't know how they were going to get around those different preferences when she retired. The house was very much his domain, but they needed to work out a way of coexisting in harmony, despite their differences. Such challenges can be tricky to overcome but having discussions can be productive. Situations are likely to be different in the future and the alternative is to carry on with how you have done things for years, at a time when circumstances were different from the new norm.

Flying solo

For retirees who are lucky enough to be a couple, then, of course, they can support each other in exploring new classes or volunteering opportunities. You can tackle the retirement challenge together.

But what about the solo retiree? Loneliness and isolation are serious issues across all ages, but especially amongst those in retirement.

Celia reminds me about the importance of establishing social networks. For many who have lived alone very happily for years while working, retirement is a significant change and not necessarily a change for the better. Celia points out how important it is to adjust to this change and create a new daily routine.

She tells me about a chap who enjoys being on his own but developed a strict routine for his retirement days. He goes to the gym three times a week, each time at 9am. After the gym, he visits Caffè Nero for his caffeine fix, and then goes to teach as a volunteer in a school. Forming a schedule like this is similar to a typical working routine with fixed hours and locations. While this gentleman loves living on his own, this forced contact with others provides a supportive framework to avoid isolation and loneliness.

Co-housing is another fantastic example of single people living with others but retaining their independence and their own way of doing things. Celia explains that you can live on your own and still have plenty of possibilities for being with people outside of your home.

Embrace the community as you define your purpose. Not only will it deliver help to others but a huge amount of help for yourself too.

Giving your time, talents and treasure

For some people, their purpose includes helping others less fortunate and having a positive impact on society. If this is important to you, you'll be interested to hear Lauren Janus' thoughts on the important questions to ask before you give money to charity.

After spending more than 15 years working in the charitable sector, Lauren started to feel a bit disillusioned with spending all her time telling donors why one charity was "absolutely the best". She soon realised that pitching one charity over another wasn't helping people understand how social change happens. There are usually a bunch of different factors involved, whether you are saving the polar bears or curing cancer.

What Lauren really wanted to do was explain how a donor can navigate the charitable landscape and give money in a way that's most meaningful to them, helping them understand how their money is impacting specific issues – that's the secret behind successful philanthropy.

At the time of our conversation, Lauren was running the charitable giving advisory service she had founded called Thoughtful Philanthropy, which helped people become more informed and better philanthropists.

Becoming informed

Like many of us, I give money to charities. And, like most people, I don't fully understand how those gifts are making a difference. What is the impact of those donations? And how much effort really went into choosing those charities? It was certainly more a decision of the heart than the head.

When we think about donating money in retirement, we have a unique opportunity to spend more time digging into the operations of each charity, as well as supporting charities with a hopefully more predictable set of finances. Lauren explains that her organisation allowed retirees to have a conversation with an adviser to discuss why they want to be more intentional about giving away their hard-earned (and saved) money. It's common to hear retirees say they want to be less haphazard with their donations.

For some in retirement, they are also thinking about larger, lasting legacies. Giving proper thought to the destination of substantial donations is hugely enlightening. In her new role, Lauren continues to advise donors of all ages and incomes and she really tries to dispel the myth that you need to be rich to be a philanthropist or a donor. And, of course, people have a wide range of passions and interests. Your charitable ambitions will be immensely personal to you, so giving money in an intentional way to two or three organisations which work directly with issues that you feel strongly about means you can make a lasting contribution in a way that makes sense to you.

It's not all about the money

Today's typical 65-year-old retiree is experiencing a hugely different life from 40 years ago. Life expectancy is typically better, along with improved health, vitality and energy, as I discuss in depth in this book. This different retirement means access to different experiences. In the UK and the US, a lot is happening to tap into this new retired skill base. Charities are better appreciating everything retirees can bring to the table, and that goes way beyond money.

Lauren explains that many people associate volunteering with helping in a charity shop or litter picking, and while these roles are important, people can make a tremendous difference through skills-based volunteering. Giving your treasure (cash donations) remains essential for charities' success but your talents are equally valuable and giving your time to a cause you feel passionate about can give you a renewed sense of purpose in retirement.

Mark Anness is a fantastic example of someone who has used his time and talents to make a real difference to the lives of others. Mark is a trustee of the charity Myra's Wells, which provides clean water to communities in Burkina Faso in West Africa. Since retiring, this role has become like a full-time job for Mark; it's become his purpose. Mark has seen first-hand the profound effect his work and the charity's wells have made. Accessible water means more children can attend school because they have more available time in their day, people can wash their clothes, the livestock is healthier and the health of the villagers has improved – there are no longer weekly bouts of sickness and diarrhoea. It truly has been life-changing for the people of Burkina Faso, and for Mark too!

If Mark's story has inspired you, perhaps think about how you could use your own time and skills to help others. Could volunteering be part of your life's purpose?

Don't stop working

Historically, older age was seen as the end point for careers. However, attitudes are changing and far more opportunity exists to continue working later into life. For some, it's a necessity. For others, it's a way of retaining their existing purpose or pursuing a new one.

Advertising legend Rory Sutherland believes that it's strange how we accept people retiring. The behavioural economics expert and Vice Chairman at Ogilvy UK explains that when someone retires from a company, they take a lifetime of accumulated knowledge, contacts, experience and instinct; they take it and they walk straight out of the door. He believes there has to be a compromise, one that acknowledges the benefit for the employer to continue to draw on your experience, your knowledge and your contacts, but where you're not required to come into work every day; you won't necessarily retain the same position of power you previously enjoyed.

Rory shares the example of Finnish Railways: "If you retire from Finnish Railways, they pay you a retainer to answer questions online. I'm obviously making up the following example, but let's say you're an engineer on Finnish Railways, then six months after you retire, there's a points failure during a period of very cold weather. They'll get in touch with you and seek your advice on how to solve a problem they know you encountered many times during your long career."

Finnish Railways realised that every time someone retired, someone else had to learn a whole load of things from scratch, but if they paid retirees a fraction of their previous salary, they could continue to draw on that experience. And that retired engineer wasn't constrained to remain living in Finland – technology gave them the freedom to live or be wherever they chose.

Rory's example illustrates that technology and a changing mindset to what retirement means no longer necessarily requires you to give up work completely.

What's more, demographic shifts mean that simply maintaining current rates of employment requires us to prepare society and the workplace for millions more older workers being gainfully employed. But are we prepared and willing to do so?

Inspired by Channel 4's documentary *Old People's Home for 4 Year Olds* (a pseudo-scientific experiment placing 11 pensioners and a group of 4-year-old children in a home together), and the experience of his father passing away, Stuart Lewis launched a digital community for the over-50s.

Rest Less aims to give its members support during one of life's biggest transitions since leaving the education system. Initially wanting to help people bridge working five days a week to doing nothing, Stuart created a guide to retirement. Then, realising that, increasingly, over-50s needed critical resources to help manage their transition, he set up a job board that hosts jobs from employers interested in an age-diverse workforce. These employment opportunities tend to have a bias towards a more flexible working pattern and the employers involved are known for their ethical values. Other features on the site include a volunteering page with an ideas and inspiration section, encouraging members to share their stories with others to inspire action. Stuart also engages in extensive press outreach, attempting to raise awareness about the outdated stereotypes around age in the workplace. He wants people to challenge their perceptions around these biases and think about age in a more positive and aspirational way.

If you're over or approaching 50, then, as Stuart explains, you are part of one of the most diverse groups of people. The transferable skills you've built up from 20, 30 or 40 years of work and life experience are immense. Just as Professor Andrew J Scott encourages us to appreciate the huge opportunities that lie ahead for people aged 50–70, Stuart urges those turning 50 to consider their 20-year plan. Viewing this time as an opportunity for personal development and exploring new careers can open up a world of possibility.

It can be quite liberating to consider what you want to do next. What role will work play in your retirement years? Have you considered how you could forge a new career path after you have 'retired' so that you don't have to retire but can instead create a better work–life balance? Will that be part of finding your purpose?

Another of my podcast guests, Victoria Tomlinson, shares Stuart's beliefs about empowering those in retirement to explore development opportunities and wants to stop ageing from being seen as a liability to society. Instead, it should be seen as a transformative force for good in the workplace.

Victoria founded Next-Up, a company working with employees over 50. When the Next-Up team starts working with people approaching the end of their careers, they often find it's the first time they've begun articulating what they want from their future. How many days do you want to work? Do you need to earn money? Do you want to make money? And what about your dreams and ambitions?

Many of the people Next-Up works with explore options, from volunteering and working in schools to non-executive directorships or trustee positions at charities and non-profit organisations, including schools. I know how important taking on a role like this was for one client and friend of mine, whose sense of self and continued connection with the world kept him current and relevant for many years after retiring. As part of Victoria's vision, she encourages the older generation to help the younger generation with their businesses through a mentoring programme. She has found this to be a significant benefit to both parties: those who have lived their work lives have created many connections they can introduce to the younger generation and the mentor gains a sense of purpose and the feel-good factor of helping someone improve their life.

What is your purpose in retirement?

Although the transition from work to retirement can be a tricky adjustment, moving into this stage of life offers many opportunities to find a renewed sense of purpose, from volunteering to building a new community. In some cases, it doesn't mean leaving work at all.

Key takeaways

- We all need a sense of purpose, regardless of our stage of life. The transition to retirement provides a perfect opportunity to reassess yours.

- More and more people are working in their retirement. Don't underestimate the value of your transferable skills; your talents and experience can open exciting doors to employment and personal development opportunities.

- Community is key for a happy and fulfilled life. It's too easy to lose your social networks when you leave work, so forming new connections is essential for building a robust bridge from working life to retirement.

- If making charitable donations forms part of your purpose, make sure you're informed on how your money will be spent. Choosing two or three charities that support causes you're intensely passionate about, rather than spreading your contributions in lots of directions, ensures you're helping make a difference in the places that are most important to you.

Having read this chapter, do you now feel you have a clear idea of what would bring meaning to your retirement, or what you need to do to get clarity?

Retirement is a big deal. As a financial planner, I spend a lot of time creating life plans with my clients. I ask those deep questions about what you didn't manage to do and who you didn't get to be. In my experience, asking these deep questions (and answering them, of course) really helps people to uncover or affirm their purpose.

From purpose, you can start to take action.

CHAPTER 7

Accelerator 3 – It's never too late

One of the most important barriers to overcome when planning for a successful retirement is giving yourself permission. You need to allow yourself to do the things you've always wanted to do.

This mindset shift sets the scene for the third accelerator of the purpose lever: **it's never too late**.

It can be hard to think beyond our known factors, those things we're so used to doing, possibly for many years. Breaking free of that familiarity can be incredibly difficult. Perhaps you've been working in the same job or profession for decades – it's familiar and almost comfortable but, deep down, you know there is something else you want to do. The very thought of making that change can be terrifying.

When I speak to people about their financial planning, I'm often giving them permission to spend their money. It sounds crazy now I write it down, but that's the reality for so many people; they believe they need my permission to spend their own hard-earned savings. And this is with people who can afford to do so. Maybe it's a symptom of a generation – I work with so many humble people. In my experience, there aren't that many successful people in the world who display arrogance like Elon

Musk. He's so flipping successful, in part, because of that arrogance, but I find that most successful people demonstrate humility.

The permission aspect is so common, whether you are seeking that tacit approval from your financial planner or a loved one. It's also your own voice telling you what you can and can't do. You might be listening to a narrative formed during childhood or based on what society expects of you. I've faced this recently in my own life when I set my sights on buying an island off the coast of Scotland. It had a helipad (I don't have a helicopter, by the way) and was completely impracticable. But I fell in love with the idea and immediately started to think about who needed to give me permission to buy it. I see so many examples of retirees who have grown up living frugally, despite having significant wealth.

Spending large amounts of money on anything is always a challenging decision. It's a decision made more complex when not supported by a clear purpose or vision. Worrying about the judgement of others can be almost paralysing, but there is nothing stopping you from making radical changes in your life at any age. Look at McDonald's founder Ray Kroc, who was 52 years old when he opened his first restaurant. Charles Darwin was 50 when he published *On the Origin of Species* (and 50 was seen as very old in 1859). Whatever you dream of doing, if it has value and significance to you, you don't require permission to do it. Whether your ambition is small or big, it's never too late to make a start.

Once you have your grand plan fixed firmly in your mind, you need to work out how on earth you will actually do it. There are probably practicalities to consider. What steps will you take to make it happen? Even the most audacious goals can be broken down into baby steps. Don't allow the scale of the challenge to deter you from getting started. If you started life today with a blank sheet of paper, what would you design? What would your ideal life look like? If you didn't face any obstacles in making that life become a reality, how would you start? Imagine I could sprinkle some magic fairy dust and give you the option to do anything you wanted, what would your life be like? What would your retirement look like? And, perhaps most importantly for getting started, what would the next 12 months look like? Start with the possibility of what could happen, because we can always deal later with the in-between stuff.

It's not too late. It's never too late.

Even if you just start with the basic elements of what you want to achieve, you can start small and build bigger in time. Taking that first step towards an ideal life in retirement is about having the energy, vision and plan or purpose. You need to have confidence in yourself.

Don't worry about the last step, only the first.

With the first step taken, you can then worry about the next, and the next. Before you know it, you will have arrived at your destination.

How do you climb Mount Everest? Unless you have a death wish, you wouldn't attempt to summit without the services of a Sherpa. Your Sherpa knows how to climb Everest. They know what the weather is going to be like at different altitudes. They know what kit you need and when to use it. But your Sherpa isn't going to climb the mountain for you. Sure, they're going to come along for the ride, but you only succeed by doing the hard work for yourself. It's the same with your grand plan: an experienced guide won't execute your plan for you, but they will serve as a catalyst for making it happen.

Patience is such an important virtue when working towards big goals in life. In all likelihood, you can afford to take time over your progress towards a significant life goal. You won't know for sure how long you have, but the probability of having enough time is on your side.

Retirement is an incredible opportunity to realise as yet unfulfilled dreams and ambitions, so ask yourself:

How comfortable am I getting out of my comfort zone and doing something completely new?

In this chapter I'll introduce you to some people who refuse to be constrained by traditional views of ageing and see retirement as an opportunity to achieve their goals. Living longer and often healthier lives gives us more time in retirement to do the things we have never done before. This extra time is a gift to be enjoyed. We have more opportunities than ever to do the things we have always dreamt of doing or maybe never even considered before.

Ready to get inspired?

It's never too late to...complete an Ironman triathlon

I loved my conversation with Irongran.

Edwina Brockelsby, known as Eddie, is the oldest female Ironman triathlete in the UK. Now at the incredible age of 79, she has completed yet another Ironman competition, a gruelling event that consists of a 2.4-mile swim, 112-mile cycle and 26.2-mile run. She is also founder of Silverfit, a charity encouraging older people to live healthier and more sociable lifestyles.

At the time of our interview, Eddie had participated in 10 Ironman triathlons, finishing with a fastest time of 16 hours and 6 minutes. It is simply astonishing, considering Eddie only learned to swim when she was 53 and took part in her first (much shorter!) triathlon at age 58. It would be easy to assume that Eddie has been sporty her whole life but this is far from true. She didn't get into fitness until her 50th birthday, after visiting Nottingham to support a friend running a marathon. Back then, Eddie knew she couldn't run a full marathon, but she thought she might manage a half – a mere 13.1 miles! Her husband responded to the plan by telling her she couldn't even run as far as Northampton, just three miles away from where they lived. Challenge accepted!

When she moved back to London following the loss of her husband of 30 years to cancer, training played a key part in Eddie's life. The triathlons came with a pre-built social network and helped create memories for her family; she and her sons have now completed races together. Eddie is a mum and a grandmother, has published her book, *Irongran: How Keeping Fit Taught Me That Growing Older Needn't Mean Slowing Down*, and has also been honoured with the British Empire Medal for services to the health and well-being of older people.

As we saw in the last chapter, when people retire, they often lose their social networks; Eddie's charity is a great way to create a new and local friendship group while staying or becoming more active. Welcoming people from the age of 45 upwards, Silverfit runs sessions in 15 different locations throughout London, offering various activities from Nordic walking and Pilates to football and cheerleading. Each activity lasts for an hour and everyone returns to a central location afterwards to meet socially. Silverfit's passionate purpose is to make ageing happier and healthier, all while having fun. It's an organisation run by older people, for older people, voicing the fact that it's never too late to adopt a happier, more social and more physically active lifestyle as you age. Eddie leads very much by example.

Even if there isn't a Silverfit session near you, you could organise to meet a reliable friend to first walk a route, slowly building up to walking faster and eventually jogging that same route.

It's clear that Eddie has found her purpose. It's never too late to start to become more active.

It's never too late to…be a serial entrepreneur

I've met with many entrepreneurs over the years, but perhaps none so prolific and passionate about their projects than Suzanne Noble, who has been a guest on the podcast three times.

Suzanne enjoyed a successful and varied career, which included PR for big entertainment brands, founding a TV company, creating a baby-sling business and launching the money and time-saving app Frugl. Then, at age 50, while attempting to join the London technology startup industry, Suzanne very quickly realised she was the oldest person doing so. She also found there was very little support for her, which led to her co-founding Advantages of Age to challenge the media narrative around ageing.

Now just north of 60, Suzanne continues on her mission of changing the ingrained ageing stereotypes, including the belief that age 65 is the trigger for retirement. Advantages of Age is based on the ethos of positive ageing and helping people manifest their ideal life, in whatever way they desire.

The pandemic took her social enterprise to a place she never expected to be – supporting people at risk of redundancy, or who had already lost their jobs. Advantages of Age also started helping those people who were thinking about self-employment as a possible next move. That's when her next idea came to fruition. Suzanne received funding and, with co-founder Mark Elliott, piloted the idea of the Startup School for Seniors, an online programme giving all the information and support needed to start your own business later in life. Startup School for Seniors supports you through the whole process of creating a freelance career, including finding your first customer, using social media and understanding the legal requirements of trading.

Suzanne has learned a lot from her students, most importantly that you absolutely can successfully start a new business in retirement. She has so many positive stories to tell, across a variety of industries. One student was a 75-year-old woman who now runs a chutney business. She developed her homemade organic vegan chutney recipes and sold them locally, thanks to the direction and support she received from the programme. Suzanne doesn't believe this lady would have otherwise had the confidence to make her passion a reality. Another student is now a consultant, using his past employment experience to support clients looking at career transitions. Suzanne herself is still launching businesses and initiatives and she is a great example of how reaching retirement age definitely does not mean you have to stop working, and may be the ideal time to become an entrepreneur!

What business would you start if you had a blank sheet of paper and the support to do so? What's stopping you?

It's never too late to…get your degree

Longer retirement life creates a beautiful opportunity for learning something new.

Dr Liz Marr, Pro-Vice-Chancellor of The Open University at the time of our podcast conversation, joined me for a chat about the opportunities for learning new things in retirement. Liz explained how positive it is when people who have spent their entire lives in the workplace then decide they want to do something for themselves. She sees people walk across the graduation stage at age 80, degree proudly grasped in hand.

Chapter 7

The idea of The Open University (OU) came from Harold Wilson in the late 1960s. When launched, it was initially named the University of the Air because it had a particular mission: to be open to people, places, methods and ideas. This founding ethos is maintained today, although different technologies are now used – learning is mainly online, and the university's reach is much broader, attracting international as well as UK-based students.

The openness of studying at the OU comes from being able to access study very flexibly, and there are no entry requirements. So if you want to study with them, you don't need to have any past qualifications, just the appropriate levels of literacy and numeracy and the desire to succeed and develop the skills you need to study. Liz told me she thinks mature students bring so much with them from their life journeys that help them better engage with their learning than fresh-faced 18 year olds who have just left school. Some retirees may feel taking on a full degree is too much. After all, studying can be quite a daunting experience for those who haven't been in education for a long time. So, for some, the goal is to further their knowledge rather than obtain full accreditation.

I am a huge fan of lifelong learning. The sense of relief so many people feel after leaving school or graduating from university, knowing they won't have to sit another exam, saddens me. Not only is challenging our brains proven to delay the onset of dementia, what learning adds to my life is enormous. A significant amount of my spare time – and working day – is taken up with learning. The topics change and my interests shift, but I have a thirst for knowledge that some would say is unquenchable! Personally, I am looking forward to the time when I can spend most of my day reading and learning!

Have you considered resuming your studies in retirement or perhaps studying for a formal qualification for the first time? After all, it's never too late! And the health benefits are vast.

It's never too late to…race across the Sahara

What's the most physically gruelling challenge you can imagine?

Dennis Hall, the founder of Yellowtail Financial Planning, chose to leave the Royal Marines after a 10-year career to work in the financial advice profession.

In his early 60s, after two very different yet successful careers, Dennis' view of retirement is pleasantly simple: if he can still be helpful, still serve people and continue learning himself, then he will keep doing what he's doing – helping people make those important financial decisions.

When Dennis turned 40, he took part in Marathon des Sables, a seven-day, 250-kilometre self-sufficient trek across part of the Sahara Desert between Morocco and Algeria. He decided to apply again at the age of 60, but Covid put a stop to his plan. Thankfully, he was able to take part the following year.

The challenge was not easy, and while some would think it was due to Dennis' age, this could not be further from the truth. A diarrhoea and vomiting bug struck the camp, meaning almost half of the participants had to take themselves out of the competition.

The second challenge to overcome was the extreme temperature – 50 degrees Celsius or hotter. Most days, the race started at 10am, with the sun already high in the sky, and many runners dropped out due to dehydration. Dennis had to carry all the kit needed for the race each day: food, his sleeping bag, survival equipment, cooking equipment, safety equipment and water, which was extremely heavy – Dennis was carrying up to three litres at a time.

He had intended to run or jog all the way around, which is what he'd done 21 years before. However, he couldn't keep his food down. Dennis managed to consume about 2,000 calories across the three days that he raced. Still, his sweat smelled of ammonia, which is indicative of burning muscle mass for energy instead of carbohydrates. Dennis' body was quite literally eating itself!

Dennis wasn't feeling great when he reached the first checkpoint. He thought he had drunk too much water, not realising his body was responding to the first wave of that sickness bug. He stopped for a while and rested, feeling good enough to finish the final 10 kilometres for that day – that pattern of feeling ill, resting and recovering continued for two days. By day three, he was feeling mentally strong but hadn't eaten anything all day. Dennis decided it was time to withdraw from the challenge, not wanting to become a liability for his teammates or the race organisers.

When I asked Dennis if withdrawing was a tough decision, especially with the Marine mentality in mind, he told me it was "the sensible decision". He was acutely aware of the consequences to himself of continuing while ill, but he also considered the risk created for others whom he might have placed in danger. Sadly, Dennis witnessed one of his fellow challengers suffer a heart attack during the race and this experience profoundly affected him. His motto of 'live for the moment' was reinforced.

He raised over £12,000 for The Royal Marines Charity, and his achievement serves as a reminder that age doesn't need to be a barrier to accomplish exceptional things, or even to attempt them. It's never too late to take on new (or old) challenges!

It's never too late to…teach

Take a moment to reflect on your career history. How many skills have you acquired, and how much knowledge have you learned? Do you really want to just head to the golf course when you have so much left to give? Now combine those skills and knowledge with your desire to contribute to society and possibly your local community. One very effective way you can bring this all together is to teach!

Katie Waldegrave, a teacher herself, met Lucy Kellaway (aged 57 at the time) soon after Katie had given birth to twins. Lucy had decided she wasn't ready to hang up her working shoes but wanted to start a second career, something different from being a hugely successful journalist for the *Financial Times*. She decided she wanted to teach.

While spending time together, they both realised that Lucy couldn't be the only person in the world who was prepared to start a new career in teaching later in life, so they founded Now Teach, an educational charity supporting people to start a career in education. Many of the people they work with have reached the stage of life where they are wanting different things out of their careers, or perhaps they have retired or experienced a key relationship shift, such as their children leaving home or being more independent.

Katie's message is simple: we need more great people in the teaching profession. What's been exciting and surprising is how many people have already considered becoming a teacher. Katie's theory is that the world is divided into two kinds of people: those with a book in them and those who want to teach. Which kind are you?

Teacher training can involve university or in-school learning, either locally or further afield. The only official prerequisite for becoming a teacher is that you need a degree. You then undertake a year of unpaid teacher training or you may qualify for a government bursary. On top of the qualifications, all you need is the right attitude and the desire to work with young people.

Katie feels that humility is a crucial requirement as it's tough to go from being excellent at something to being inexperienced in a new career. In theory, you might understand that you will start from the bottom; in practice, that can be quite a shock to the system! Teaching is a very different profession from most. For those who love it, it can be rejuvenating – learning to be an excellent teacher can inject new life into older candidates.

Could you harness your skills and experience to empower young people to have a better education? If you've always loved the idea of teaching but you thought it was too late to start a new career, think again!

It's never too late for you!

The people in this chapter show what is truly possible when you are open to change and trying new things. I hope the stories I've shared have inspired you to believe that age really is just a number and retirement doesn't have to mean giving up on your dreams – it's the perfect time to fulfil your ambitions and create new ones.

Chapter 7

It really is never too late!

> **Key takeaways**
>
> - Reaching the national age of retirement doesn't mean you have to give up work if you don't want to. More and more people are using this next chapter of their life to explore the world of entrepreneurship, academia or even start a brand-new career.
>
> - If getting fit is your priority later in life, you can improve your fitness at any age. Retirement is a great time to prioritise your physical health, take up a new sport, or challenge yourself to try something out of your comfort zone.
>
> - Once you've decided what it's never too late for, create a plan for how you will make it happen. Breaking down your big goals into smaller, practical steps can create a clear pathway to making your vision a reality.

Remember the pyramid model I shared in Chapter 2 with the four zones of retirement? The people in this chapter who realised it's never too late to do something important to them are certainly not just drifting through their retirement. They've grasped their unfulfilled dreams with both hands and are making them a reality, striving for the pinnacle of the pyramid to truly thrive in this phase of life.

Sometimes, there are barriers to taking that first step that seem insurmountable at first glance. So, enlist the help of a Sherpa – a financial life planner, a coach or someone who's already been there and done what it is you're burning to do. Secure that permission, whether it's a reassuring nod from someone you care about, or the voice inside your own head.

Then ask yourself: what is it you've always wanted to do, but not had the time, confidence or resources to do? What's the first step you can take to make it happen? Who can support you on your journey? If you were opening this book again in just 12 months' time, what would you like to have in your life?

Remember, the early retirement years are likely to be when you have the most vitality. So while it's never too late, things can become more challenging as you head into later life. Why not start today?

Self-care

CHAPTER 8

Accelerator 4 – The science of living better for longer

Let's talk about your brain.

Imagine drawing a line from where you are today through to age 100. Let's say you're 62 now and your average life expectancy is 85. At some point, you're going to drop off that line. It might not happen at the time of your average life expectancy; your demise could happen sooner or later. But dropping off that line, at some point, is inevitable.

When you learn to ski, you start on a green slope, with its gentle incline. Then, you move to a blue slope and a bit more of a challenge. You progress through a red slope, then a black and then, ultimately, head off-piste, for the most challenging skiing conditions. That's a little like your life. In your 20s and 30s, you're on the green slope of life. As you move into your 40s, you head onto the blue slope. By the time your 50s and 60s come around, you're on the red slope of life, before entering the black slope in your 70s and 80s.

Eventually, you come off-piste.

People acknowledge that, as they get older, they're going to decline in mental function. What can you do to enhance that inevitable period in your life? What steps can you take today to give yourself the best possible chance of living a longer, healthier, happier life?

As we move to the second lever of self-care, the first accelerator to explore is **the science of living better for longer**.

When I have conversations with clients in their 90s, it's noticeable that they struggle a little to keep up with some concepts. But everyone's experience of ageing is unique.

One client of mine, a very bright chap, has always selected his own investments. He's done reasonably well over the years, and done so in his own way. But, as he grew older, he started to experience the symptoms of Parkinson's disease. There's a physical outcome from Parkinson's but also a mental decline typically associated with the condition. Making investment decisions became harder as the disease progressed but, fortunately, he recognised this limitation and made the sensible choice to delegate financial decisions at the right time. Not everyone does.

In my experience, the people who stay sharpest as they get older are those most connected with some form of commerce. It's great to stay active as you get older, but walking the dog and meeting friends for coffee are unlikely to make a significant contribution to your mental acuity in retirement. I see clients who lead a life of leisure and seem to be drifting away mentally. Instead of getting their information and ideas first-hand, they are consuming it from the *Daily Mail* or from friends on the golf course.

Leisure activities in retirement rarely expose us to cultural challenges, or other perspectives. We risk entering an echo chamber of sorts. It's in stark contrast to your working life, when you are faced with pretty much everything on a regular basis, dealing with colleagues, bosses, customers and everyone else. You're making meaningful decisions.

If I could wave a magic wand and help you design your ideal retirement, it should include a plan to maintain and even enhance your cognitive function. Doing something that's real and relevant is key to a successful retirement, in my experience. You need to do more than gardening. Even volunteering can help, when it happens at the right level.

The difference between those who continue to be engaged in retirement and those who don't is clear.

I've got one client who established a successful family business, building it from one shop to an entire nationwide chain. When he sold his business to a larger company, he took on non-executive board positions and kept working at a senior level. He's sharp as a tack, despite his advancing years. Serving on the board of a large business means he remains engaged with the day-to-day challenges faced by the organisation. It's helping his brain.

Another client retired from the business he set up with his son, but stepped away entirely. He's become disconnected from that world and it shows. While he is by no means 'old' yet, he's noticeably slowing down in terms of his decision-making and mental acuity, something I see time and again.

Another client, now in his mid-80s, continues to run his insurance brokerage. He lost his wife to cancer years ago but still goes into the office each morning. And that sense of purpose keeps him and his brain going.

If you're retiring *from* something, make sure you're retiring *to* something. You need to find something in retirement that is going to occupy and challenge your brain. However, you must also accept that your brain will change as you get older. I've seen examples of people holding on to certain roles and responsibilities for a bit longer than they should have done. One notable study from RUSH University found that financial literacy declines with age, but confidence in financial decision-making does not. With increasingly complex financial decisions to make in retirement, this can be a potent combination of reduced ability and static confidence. Working with an expert guide who can support your financial decision-making is key.

How we age has become a hot topic in scientific research. New findings shed light on what happens to our brains and bodies as we get older. The thinking now is that ageing is about all of life, not just the end of life. In fact, according to Professor Sir Muir Gray, who we'll meet later, we're constantly training for later life. In his 70s, Sir Muir told me about a bus journey he took in London when a kind young lady offered him a seat. He politely declined, explaining he was in training. When she asked whether he was a cyclist, he explained, to much amusement, that he was in training for his 80s and 90s!

So before we dive into this accelerator topic – the science of living better for longer – consider the following question:

How much do you know about the science of ageing and what steps can you take to stay fit and well in retirement?

In this chapter I'll share the latest research and ideas about how we age. This accelerator aims to help you make informed decisions about how you live so you can look after yourself and your brain as best you can throughout your retirement.

What a neuroscientist can tell us about ageing

Certain myths exist relating to old age and how our brains work, not least the big misconception that memory always declines with age. Dr Daniel Levitin, a psychologist, musician, neuroscientist and author, tells me this is just not true. He explains we can expose this myth by realising older people often blame Alzheimer's if they lose their phone or forget their computer password. However, 20 year olds are doing the same thing regularly.

What is true, however, is that at around age 60, neurochemical changes occur in our brains, modifying the neurostructure. These changes make us less likely to want to try new things and to become a little more complacent generally. However, we can fight these changes with effort and determination, with plentiful rewards including better health, increased lifespan, more pleasure and better engagement with life.

Another common myth is that you stop growing new neurons and, consequently, new connections in the brain, known as neural pathways. This cannot be further from the truth. We are developing new neurons constantly until the moment of our death. Each time you learn something new, a neural pathway is constructed. Building up these new neural pathways creates something essential: cognitive reserve. The critical task for the over-60s is to build up enough brain pathways so that, if things start to go wrong due to disease or age-related atrophy, there is so much reserve that the decline is not so noticeable.

It's undeniably harder to learn as you age, because the brain is configured to be maximally flexible during the first 12 years of life. However, you can keep your brain active by immersing yourself in new activities. For example, if you have enjoyed doing crosswords for the past 20 years, the pleasure you derive from doing so has little benefit to your brain. You need to push yourself out of your comfort zone, try new things, maybe Sudoku or chess for a change, and create those new pathways while opening your mind to a new way of thinking.

Daniel is an excellent model of leading by example. At age 58, while researching for his book *Successful Aging: A Neuroscientist Explores the Power and Potential of Our Lives*, he pushed himself out of his comfort zone. Despite a terrible fear of heights, he trained to become a pilot and successfully obtained his licence. Also, realising he had never accomplished his desire to play music professionally, he started writing songs and has since released an album and been on tour. You don't have to do anything as daring and challenging as Daniel, but following his guiding principle sounds sensible.

Daniel sums it up nicely: you can shift, and you can shift at any age.

Understanding and improving brain health

Dr Ben Webb has been a part of a movement over the past 15 years improving people's well-being. He is fascinated with brain health, specifically helping us understand and prevent mental decline and prevent dementia as we age.

During our conversation he tells me, "Nearly all of us have the pathology of Alzheimer's inside our brain already. In our 30s and 40s, it's already there. Whether it's going to manifest into symptoms of cognitive decline later in life is difficult to predict."

It may surprise you to know that whether or not the disease progresses is largely within our control. Ben explains there are six pillars that can reduce our risk of mental decline and improve our well-being. They're well worth understanding so you can take control of your own brain health.

1. **Look after your medical health.** This includes reducing high blood pressure, maintaining a healthy weight and managing diabetes. Diabetes is a very high-risk factor: the brain is the most energy-demanding organ in the body, using 20% of the body's total energy, and it uses glucose to draw on that energy. When diabetic people become insulin resistant, the brain isn't being fuelled properly. Taking care of your physical health to avoid developing these conditions is the first step.

2. **Follow a diet for a healthy brain and gut.** Ideally, this is a Mediterranean-style diet that's high in vegetables and fruits. Eating cruciferous and green leafy vegetables, like broccoli, kale and spinach, can reduce your chances of mental decline by up to about 30%. That's got to be a simple change to make.

3. **Strive for an active lifestyle.** Incorporating regular movement into your daily routine will improve a range of abilities, including clarity of thinking, mental reasoning and memory. In fact, according to Ben, a recent research study shows that vigorous walking for just 20 to 30 minutes every day reduces your chances of mental decline by 30%. Aerobic exercise supplies your brain with continuous blood flow, containing all the nutrients your brain needs, but it also promotes the growth of new brain cells in the same areas affected by Alzheimer's and dementia.

4. **Manage uncontrolled stress.** Neuroscience has shown that uncontrolled stress is just as damaging to your brain as excessive alcohol consumption. It shrinks the parts of the brain involved in memory and learning – those parts that are affected by Alzheimer's and dementia. To a certain level, stress is a good thing, but too much uncontrolled or chronically elevated stress can cause real problems for your brain health. Meditation and mindfulness are very effective ways of managing your stress levels.

5. **Have regular and restorative sleep.** Not getting the recommended amount and quality of sleep can trigger secondary consequences for general health and, specifically, brain health. There are two reasons why sleep is so important for your brain health throughout life: firstly, when you sleep, memories are laid down; experiences of the day before are integrated into the memory sentences in the brain and combined with stored older, long-term memories. Secondly, when you're sleep deprived, you're interrupting that process, which can lead to memory issues later in life. While you sleep, a sort of 'deep-cleaning' team goes to work in the brain overnight. This deep-cleaning team washes away, amongst other metabolic waste, the toxic proteins that are associated with, and very likely the cause of, Alzheimer's disease.

So, when the full complement of seven to eight hours of sleep every night is not met, not just day after day, but week after week, year after year, perhaps decade after decade, those proteins accumulate inside the brain, leading to the disease process for Alzheimer's and manifesting as symptoms.

6. **Complete complex activities that challenge and engage your brain.** We need to try different activities as we age to ensure our brains continue to lay down new neural pathways. As Dr Daniel Levitin says, "It's protection for the brain; you're building up a buffer of neurons – a cognitive reserve, allowing you to access memories via a number of different routes, should some become compromised as you age. This is one of the best ways you can protect your brain as you get older."

Looking after your brain health is one important part of staying healthier for longer, but one thing we know for sure is that your vitality will also decrease. Thankfully, there are some steps you can take to combat the decline to some degree.

A prescription for a healthy retirement

How many press-ups can you do? Hold onto your answer for a moment.

According to Professor Sir Muir Gray, we need to change our view of ageing and what is happening to us as we live longer. Renowned public health pioneer Sir Muir is helping people, including those in the medical profession, understand that ageing alone is not the cause of significant problems, at least not until we reach our late 90s. Instead, problems we often associate with ageing tend to come from the loss of fitness. What's more, many diseases associated with age are often preventable. When we spoke, Sir Muir said that challenging these negative attitudes and beliefs is the most difficult thing about ageing.

Ageing is a normal biological process. It has two effects: firstly, getting older reduces our maximum level of ability. For example, Roger Federer noticed his maximum heart rate was starting to decline from age 38 onwards. Secondly, ageing reduces our resilience, which is best described as our 'reserve' or how we bounce back and cope with exertion, however mild.

Paradoxically, the more you are affected by ageing, the more activity you need. You should be doing more the older you are. And as you accumulate long-term health conditions, some of which can limit your mobility, you need to become even more active. More activity will help prevent disease, as well as improve your response to medical treatment. That's where the question about press-ups comes in – Sir Muir believes that everyone should be able to do the same number of press-ups as their age. But mostly, Sir Muir believes we need to encourage people to be optimistic. People need to stay physically active and emotionally and cognitively fit as they age.

It's common for doctors to prescribe medication to treat long-term health conditions, perhaps along with some diet recommendations, but Sir Muir believes they should be prescribing activity too. The National Activity Therapy Service is an initiative set up to support this vision: when someone is given a drug prescription, they will also be given an activity prescription. It is based on what Sir Muir calls the Five S Programme: strength, stamina, suppleness and skill, with the fifth 's' being psychological.

Having worked in the NHS for over 40 years, Sir Muir is well placed to develop and implement solutions. In recent years, he has introduced the NHS Ageing Well programme, the Learning Programme and the Live

Longer Better programme. These initiatives enable people to live longer, reduce the need for health and social care and reverse the negative effects of lockdown. Within these programmes, Sir Muir works with physical activity professionals and exercise physiologists, who are currently mainly focusing on younger people, which is very important for prevention. But there is also a necessity to work with the older generation so that they can live their lives better and for longer. He's encouraging people to ask for new trainers instead of chocolates on those milestone 60th, 70th or 80th birthdays!

Excessive sitting syndrome

Sir Muir is the author of several books, including *Sod 70!: The Guide to Living Well* and *Sod Sitting, Get Moving!: Getting Active in Your 60s, 70s and Beyond*, designed to encourage us to shift our attitude towards ageing and keep moving for longer. When we spoke for the podcast, he challenged me by saying I was probably doing a dangerous thing right now – sitting down! He was right.

If you're approaching retirement, Sir Muir calculates that you have been sitting down for 15 years of your life already, potentially with another 30 years of sitting ahead of you as you become less mobile. While some will have no choice but to be chairbound, technology offers some exciting possibilities. For example, we could use virtual reality to get people 'out of the house' and socialising with others. With virtual reality, you could meet up with friends and (virtually) cycle from Land's End to John O'Groats together, perhaps for 30 minutes a day, chatting to each other as you go.

Before his heart attack, Sir Muir used to go running. But now, he stretches for 10 minutes every morning, walks briskly, cycles every day and is toying with the idea of getting an electric bike to tackle the big hills in his home city, Oxford. According to Sir Muir, the evidence points towards using the same energy when riding an electric bike as a manual one, as you go further, faster!

The evidence is mounting and momentum is building behind the idea that we have a significant amount of control over how we age. So why not take a leaf out of Sir Muir's book and get down on the floor for those press-ups…

Slowing down the ageing process

Ageing starts at birth. The only difference is that ageing starts manifesting much more when we reach 60 to 65. As we've heard, our metabolic function, brain function and other organs begin to slow down.

Slowing down the ageing process is surely the holy grail. But is it really possible? Dr Jitka Vseteckova, a senior lecturer in health and social care at the OU, believes there are steps we can take that could help.

Jitka explains that to prevent massive or very rapid slowing down of functions and problems associated with reaching this age, we must focus specifically on what we don't want to lose. There is no way to stop the ageing process, but there is a way to prevent a steep ageing curve.

There are two ways of viewing the ageing process: normal physiological ageing, which is what most people experience as their body and brain start to show signs of getting older, and pathological ageing. This is where some neurodegenerative conditions (for example, some forms of dementia) impact the way our neurons transmit the information necessary for us to function well in life, which often results in creating a barrier or a difficulty.

Jitka explains that it's important to exercise those muscles to reduce the impact. Of course, we all forget things every now and then, like where we left the keys and, as we heard from Dr Daniel Levitin, this is all normal. But as long as we can remember that we forgot something, it's all fine. The problem starts when we cannot remember that we forgot. Then the impact on our day-to-day life begins.

Jitka has created four core pillars of healthy ageing, which are strikingly – and reassuringly – similar to Ben's six pillars of brain health.

1. **Nutrition:** it's key to eat regularly and include all macronutrients – carbohydrates, proteins and fats – in your diet. This keeps your

muscles and metabolism healthy and provides vital nutrients to your organs, including the brain.

2. **Physical activity:** staying active is important to maintain your muscle tone as you get older. This can be anything from doing chores for 20 minutes every day, walking up and down the stairs or doing some gardening.

3. **Hydration:** your body needs about 1.5 litres of fluids per day – ideally water – to carry out its metabolic processes.

4. **Social and cognitive stimulation:** these are important for combatting isolation, which can be a big issue in retirement, particularly for those in the latter stages and living alone.

Maybe ageing well isn't such a challenge, if there are just a few big rocks to focus on?

How can science help you live better for longer?

Ageing is something that happens throughout our lives, not just in retirement, but as we get later on in life, we're more likely to encounter some of the health challenges we typically associate with getting older. As this chapter has shown, 21st-century science provides many opportunities to learn more about what happens to our health as we age and how we can improve our chances of living a longer and healthier retirement.

> ### Key takeaways
>
> - As we get older, neurochemical changes in the brain reduce our desire to try new things. However, we can override these feelings with determination and effort. When we learn a new skill, it leads to new neural pathways being formed, creating better brain health.
>
> - Research has shown there are lots of things we can do to improve our brain health. Following a healthy diet, staying

> active, managing stress levels, improving our sleep hygiene and keeping our brains active with new activities can all help reduce the risk of mental decline.
>
> - Many of the health issues associated with older age are, in fact, a result of reduced activity levels. Regular exercise and maintaining an active lifestyle can reduce the chance of mental decline, as well as long-term health conditions like type 2 diabetes.

The science helping us live better for longer is evolving at a rate of knots. From what I've shared in this chapter, how well do you feel you are currently implementing the suggestions shared by my expert guests to optimise your brain health as you age?

- Are you taking steps to keep moving and reduce the likelihood of developing diseases often associated with later life?

- Are you eating the right kinds of food to give your brain and body the best chance of flourishing for longer?

- Are you keeping stresses under control?

- Are you getting the right amount of sleep to allow your brain to recover and replenish overnight?

- And what about challenging your brain, keeping mentally engaged with the world and trying new things?

- Are there areas you need to focus on to give yourself the best chance of thriving mentally and physically?

The decisions you need to make as you enter and progress through retirement are not insignificant. In Chapters 10 and 13 I delve deeper into the implications of losing mental capacity and the complexity of needing care. Needless to say, these are situations you would wish to avoid, so take heed from the experts I've introduced you to and start to take control of your future today.

CHAPTER 9

Accelerator 5 – Taking control of your health and well-being

The expert conversations I've shared so far in this book clearly illustrate one point: you need to take control of your future. Some have already suggested ways of doing so and taking the reins on your health, physically and mentally, is advice often associated with living a successful retirement.

My second accelerator for the self-care lever is **taking control of your health and well-being**.

It's all too easy to allow the natural physical and mental decline that comes with age to happen, without any attempt at intervention. When I look at the clients I meet, and others who are living in retirement, I can see patterns. I can see what many people appear to be getting wrong.

Maintaining physical health in retirement places a lot of emphasis on movement – walking, running and generally staying active. We're constantly told we should be getting our 10,000 steps a day to stay healthy but I'm convinced there is another, complementary, approach: go to the gym and lift weights.

The steps as well? Yes, it's definitely helpful. But having read around this subject and interviewed experts in the field, I am convinced that maintaining your strength as you age is a significant indicator of a successful retirement.

Why do I feel so strongly about this? Our muscle mass naturally declines with age and that decline robs you of your future vitality. Each year, unless you intervene, you become weaker. Our muscle mass declines by approximately 3% to 8% each decade from age 30 onwards. The rate of decline is higher after age 60 and this decline in muscle mass is a major cause of disability in older people. The weaker we become, the more potential we have to suffer longer term from an accident or fall, or be hospitalised.

Keeping fit, active and strong in retirement brings with it another benefit: it helps us form and maintain connections with other people. When we keep our bodies fit and healthy, we generally end up meeting other people who are on a similar journey. Finding and joining groups who share this goal of keeping active will expose you to like-minded souls. Social connection is a significant influence on your longevity, so anything you can do to avoid becoming socially isolated in retirement is likely to improve your outcomes.

We all know someone elderly who has taken a tumble. What happens next is often the result of their strength. If you're strong, you can probably stay out of hospital; if you're not, you're more likely to end up in hospital following a fall. Your prognosis is then likely to be worse. The older you get, the more serious the impact of injuries from falls, as they result in fractures and hospitalisation. According to the NHS, falls are a major cause of emergency hospital admissions for older people, and lead to many moving from their own home into residential care. Unsurprisingly, those at the highest risk of falls are the over-65s.

Women in particular often don't consider lifting weights a desirable activity: they don't want to 'bulk up'. But weightlifting is an even more important activity for women because their bone density decreases faster than men's. Lifting weights stresses your bones (as well as your muscles) and can help stave off osteoporosis. One study found that post-menopausal women who took part in a strength training programme for a year experienced significant increase in their bone density in the spine and hips. It's these two parts of the body that are most affected by osteoporosis in older women.

Living longer is brilliant, as long as those extra years are healthy. We all know that prevention is always better than cure, so the more you keep moving and maintain a healthy lifestyle, the more likely you will enjoy a longer life.

When it comes to your own physical and mental fitness, **how in control of your health and well-being are you?**

In this chapter you will find snippets from my conversations with some of the most fascinating and inspiring people I have had the privilege of interviewing for the podcast. They share how they take control of their health in retirement and their motivations for doing so. As you read about this accelerator, you will discover that individual preferences differ. But common threads allow these guests to keep as fit, strong and healthy as possible while maintaining their vitality.

Within this topic of taking control of your health and well-being, I will also explore isolation and loneliness and how these significant issues accelerate a physical decline in later life. And I'll look at the steps you can take to maintain your mental health – which is arguably as important as your physical well-being.

Taking control in the face of illness and adversity

Every so often, you come across someone in life who is, quite simply, inspirational. Kevin Webber is one of those people. Back in 2014, life seemed to be ticking along nicely for Kevin until something happened that shook his world. He was diagnosed with terminal prostate cancer.

Not willing to accept his fate without a fight, Kevin did what he knew how to do best: he put one foot in front of the other and started running. It's fair to say he's never stopped to look back. Instead, he's used his diagnosis and drive to remain fit and well and raise thousands of pounds for Prostate Cancer UK, becoming one of their leading spokespeople and fundraisers. What's more, he has written a book called *Dead Man Running: One Man's Story of Running to Stay Alive*.

When Kevin received his diagnosis he was convinced that, because everyone he'd spoken to had been cured, he was in the same camp. However, when he stepped into his doctor's office in November 2014 he was told the cancer had spread to other parts of his body, and it was growing fast. He was given two years, three to four if he was lucky. At 49 years old, he was expecting, one day, to watch his nine-year-old son do his A-levels, be a grandad and drive around Europe in his retirement. Suddenly, those plans and dreams were taken away from him. For Kevin, life was already over.

However, Kevin's wife has a great expression that was key in helping him cope: "If you wake up in the morning, and you feel okay, it's going to be a good day."

Prostate cancer explained

No one knows why you get prostate cancer. It is hereditary in part but not always and, if you're Black, you have a higher risk. One in eight men in the UK are diagnosed with prostate cancer – it's the cancer most affecting British men. 82% of men diagnosed with the condition will be cured but having said that, a man dies from the disease every 45 minutes in the UK.

Kevin describes how the prostate works: "As men get older, their prostates grow; there's nothing wrong with that. The prostate is right next to the bladder, so when it naturally grows in older age (we're talking over-50s), it will push against the bladder, which is why a lot of older men get up at night for a wee. However, if you have a tumour on your prostate and it's on the side of the prostate next to the bladder, then that will push on the bladder and make you need the toilet. That's why no man should think, 'Oh, I'm only going to have another wee, my prostate is simply growing.' Instead, they should think, 'It's unlikely, but possible, that I have early-stage prostate cancer. Let's get it checked out.'"

Kevin explains that his cancer started growing on the other side of the prostate, so by the time he was getting up in the night for the toilet, the tumour had grown all the way through the prostate. On biopsy, all of his prostate was cancerous.

What Kevin did next is remarkable.

Taking control

Looking out the window one day, he realised he had a choice. Kevin describes it as an epiphany: "I could either give up on everything now and be a victim, or I could fight."

In his experience, the people who are given a couple of years to live and deal with it through drinking every night, eating unhealthily and never exercising because they don't see the point, often don't make it to two years. Kevin decided to deal with his cancer differently. He recognised the element of control that he had over his future.

Kevin explains: "It is important to make yourself as strong as possible. Exercise helps you tolerate chemotherapy better and generally makes it work better as well." For Kevin, this meant a return to running. He had always been a keen runner and the week before his diagnosis, he had run 20 miles. However, when he tried now, he could only manage three. Kevin remembers: "I felt really sick and I felt absolutely shattered. But also elated."

He realised that he could still run – a different kind of running, but he could still run: "I could buy a running magazine, then I could buy some new shoes, and I could look at a race maybe next month. And in the short term, I could still have a plan, as opposed to just giving up on everything." By taking this step-by-step approach, Kevin's ability to dream gradually started to return.

Wise words

Kevin advocates living in the now, chasing your dreams and not giving up. And that's what he has done ever since. He recalls: "I got to know about 20 men who were diagnosed either a year before or a year after me with the same cancer as me, in the same situation. They're all now dead apart from one – funnily enough, that guy runs as well." Kevin explains how some people he has met feel hopeless when they have any sort of problem in life – what's the point in taking a small step because the small steps are not enough? But actually, that step might be the one that makes a massive difference.

Kevin is a truly inspiring example of someone who's made the best of his health into his 50s, in spite of his cancer diagnosis. I was genuinely emotional at the end of our conversation.

I will leave you with Kevin's wise, humble words:

"If you're facing ill health, just worry about what's in front of you. A lot of things in life are about mental challenges. When things get hard, and you want to jack it in, that's when you need to just get up and go again. Because if you do, the mental rewards you get from completing a task are massive."

In Kevin's case, it's not only the mental rewards he's received, but the thousands of pounds he's raised for Prostate Cancer UK. What a difference he will make to many older people's lives.

Never too old to lift

Chris Tiley is a physiotherapist based in Birmingham. After observing his older clients' experiences of pain and suffering, he developed a passion for strength training as therapy and its benefits for the over-60s. This led to him writing his book, *Never Too Old To Lift: 8 Steps to Create Your First 12-Week Strength Training Program*, and a blog of the same name.

As I mentioned, I am a big fan of strength training myself and regularly work with coaches in sport and other areas of my life, so I really enjoyed chatting with Chris about his book and what he's learned about the benefits of strength training as we age.

Chris has developed a particular passion for introducing strength training to people who never thought it was possible. He's seen fantastic results through not only what they can do in the gym, but also how it impacts their life outside the gym.

Use it or lose it

We know that muscle strength declines from the age of 30. But Chris explains that if we take specific actions, we can counter that decline. And not only can we slow it down, we can actually reverse it; we can regain strength that we've already lost. Now that's great news!

The problem is this decline gradually creeps in. If you're particularly sporty, you may start to find the sports you have been doing become a bit more difficult; you might get more aches or niggling injuries that take longer to recover from. Chris often finds those people then give up that particular sport or take an easier option. However, these activities were actually maintaining your strength and once you stop, the decline accelerates until you find you're not able to do any of the things you used to enjoy. Chris' aim is to help those people to turn their situation around.

Strength training 101

Chris confirms my belief that most people focus on the aerobic side of exercising but ignore the strength. According to the World Health Organization, everyone should be doing at least two sessions of muscle strengthening a week. If you look at the guidelines more closely, that's for people aged 18–64. For those 65-plus, it should be three sessions.

According to Chris, there's a particular way we need to work our muscles for strength training to be effective – you need to push your muscles to the point of fatigue and ideally with 15 repetitions of an exercise.

Chris explains repetitions and sets for those who are not familiar:

A **repetition** (rep) is one single exercise performed all the way through, for example a squat. If you do 10 squats in a row, you've completed 10 repetitions.

We would call these 10 repetitions a **set**. If you were to have a short break and then do another 10 squats, you would have completed two sets of 10.

Chris explains that to get maximum benefit, the final repetition you do should be almost the last one you can manage. If you get to 10 and could have easily managed another five, you need to increase the resistance or the exercise won't be as effective at making you stronger.

For some exercises your bodyweight might be enough to create the required resistance. For others, you'll need some form of external resistance. That could be weights, for example a dumbbell or kettlebell if you're in a gym, or a rucksack filled with bottles of water or heavy books if you're at home.

Let's talk about motivation

It can be a real mental effort to get going, either in the gym or at home. Even I feel that some days, and I think I'm pretty self-motivated. On a day when you're feeling low in the motivation department, it's easy to say, "I'll leave it until tomorrow." A phrase that you repeat the next day…and the next. Before you know it, a week of not doing any exercise has passed and you end up quitting.

The more you can think about motivational barriers in advance and create strategies, the easier it is to avoid it becoming an issue. Chris recommends identifying your motivations for wanting to train, working out where you're going to do it and then creating a plan.

Ask yourself:

What exercises am I going to do?

How can I make progress over a period of time?

This approach works because it limits the mental effort required to decide what to do each day – you just refer to your plan and off you go! Chris advises designing your own, ideally with the help of a professional, rather than following ready-made programmes online, because there is no one-size-fits-all in strength training. If there's an exercise on the plan you can't do, you're more likely to skip it, rather than adapt it. The more you skip, the less effective the plan.

There's a clear similarity between strength training and personal finance. Chris says, "No one really enjoys saving or investing money. Most people enjoy spending money far more. But to spend money later in life, you need to do some saving and investing today. I see strength training as a form of investment to allow you to spend your retirement doing physical activities you enjoy."

Even if strength training doesn't float your boat, Chris' persuasive arguments of the benefits may just enable you to lift a few weights so you can look forward to doing more of the things you want in the future.

Keep on moving

Move it or Lose it

Julie Robinson is an award-winning fitness expert, who has dedicated her career to motivating thousands of people to keep active in retirement. She has done this not only by being the fitness expert for a couple of women's magazines, but over the past 12 years she has run Move it or Lose it!, the company she founded to actively help older people get moving.

In our conversation, Julie shares the story behind her hugely successful enterprise, how it works and the scientific evidence behind the importance of maintaining our strength, balance and flexibility as we age.

For some of Julie's clients, it's a case of getting them moving, especially those who don't enjoy exercise or going to the gym but would benefit from movement as they get older. Julie says, "We've always had this kind of culture that says you need to take it steady when you get older, especially after retirement, when actually the opposite is true." The research shows we need to be moving more, not less, as we clock up those years, as we heard from Chris with regard to increasing the amount of strength training we do.

However, there are many people who are frightened of exercise, which is how Move it or Lose it! came about. Julie is trying to change the widely held perception that exercise equals pain, by making it fun. She encourages routines to music, adapting them according to the group, which is a great motivational tool and really helps people get into the flow of each session. Julie says, "Recent research from Loughborough University shows music can help us release not just the usual 'happy hormones' like endorphins, but also endocannabinoids, which is like nature's own cannabis! So it's a fantastic way to relieve pain and to give yourself a legal high. I mean, what could be better?"

Most of the people who join Move it or Lose it! are in their 70s, 80s, 90s, or even hundreds. The classes are based around four cornerstones of what Julie believes helps keep us healthy as we age: flexibility, aerobics, balance and strength (FABS). The exercises can be taught seated, so anyone can take part and still get the feeling of being part of a group. This sociability aspect is key and if you can stay active, you can keep socialising – it's a virtuous circle.

Julie and her team have found another way to increase the accessibility and social reach of her classes: they've created an online community. The uptake has been remarkable, particularly among men who feel less comfortable joining in-person sessions. Julie also trains new instructors to lead the Move it or Lose it! classes and has found many older women interested in developing the skills and taking on a new role later in life. Many are worried about becoming isolated and losing their identity after they retire, so Move it or Lose it! allows them to maintain those vital social connections – a theme we keep returning to throughout this book!

Moving for joy

The importance of staying active as we get older is something The Joy Club founder Hannah Thomson also identified. She watched her gran deteriorate quickly after a dementia diagnosis and was struck by how little we do as a society to encourage an active lifestyle for those early on in their retirement.

People often dream about the lifestyle they want to have when they retire. Unfortunately, as we get older, our health starts to impact our ability to live the life we want to live. But what if we could prevent or defer those age-related illnesses to extend the number of years lived in good health? This desire is why I was keen to interview Hannah for the podcast.

As Hannah's gran's condition progressed, more and more products and support services became available to her. And while Hannah was grateful at the time, on reflection she realised we need to be doing more as a society to support people to stay happy and active early on in their retirement so that those healthy years last for longer. Hannah decided to take action and created The Joy Club, a membership site that offers discounts on a wide variety of activities, enabling people to have a joyful and social retirement.

Hannah spoke to over a hundred people to understand their experiences of retirement. She found that some retirees were having a great time, but others weren't.

She identified three key challenges that they were facing:

1. **Budget**. A lot of people she spoke to dreamt of an amazing retirement but when they got there, they realised that unlimited time on a limited budget can be a recipe for boredom.

2. **Purpose**. Many people struggled with identity loss after retiring. They found the structure, meaning and purpose they'd had in their working lives had disappeared.

3. **Loneliness**. Feeling lonely and isolated was another recurring theme for people who had lost the social networks they had formed through their jobs.

The Joy Club tries to address these issues by offering something very special. It supports those on a limited budget – people can save money without missing out. When it comes to purpose, The Joy Club offers personalised activity recommendations, including volunteering opportunities to support that sense of meaning in people's everyday lives. Finally, when people join The Joy Club they become part of a thriving community, where they can interact with other members and take part in interactive events.

It's clear The Joy Club is doing a great job at supporting people early on in retirement to stay active, happy and connected for longer.

Moving gently

Keeping fit and healthy isn't just about fitness classes or going to the gym. An advocate of the practice for over 30 years, Mark Peters says: "Tai chi is a balanced approach to life; it helps you be more aware of where you are in space. It keeps you fit and strong." Tai chi is an excellent exercise as we get older to improve balance and mobility, and it's not affected by age or medical conditions.

Mark was approached by the NHS to use his knowledge of tai chi in rehabilitation programmes for amputees, people who are wheelchair-bound, those with bad knees, backs, shoulders and arthritis, and others who need help with muscle tone. They conducted a comparative study comparing the benefits of tai chi and Zumba, expecting to find that tai chi improves your balance and relaxation and Zumba your cardio. However, they discovered that tai chi was just as aerobic as Zumba.

Mark explain that when patients undertake rehabilitation, they usually begin with circuit training to try and strengthen their muscles, but if they aren't used to exercising, then when they get on the treadmill, anxiety can set in. With tai chi, the focus is on balance, relaxation, the movement and natural breathing – you move and coordinate with your breath. Mark found that, compared to being on a treadmill or a bike, even when he made tai chi quite active, the patients' oxygen levels didn't desaturate.

And the benefits don't stop there. The outcomes of Mark's programme, Prevention for Falls, show there is a 12% improvement with general exercise, a 20–25% improvement through specific balance exercises and 43% improvement through practising tai chi. Marks says, "Tai chi is a gentle way of exercising – you don't get the lactic acid or the pain that comes back in muscles you haven't used for a long time. They will ache, but they will get stronger."

Chapter 9

Some people are interested in tai chi as an art form – the philosophy, martial applications and weapons. However, just practising it as an exercise will benefit your health; your balance, mobility and even your circulation will improve. It's a fantastic exercise for anyone of any age and maybe something you could add to your toolkit for a healthy retirement.

Taking control of the menopause

One specific group of people who benefit from taking control of their health and well-being as they get older are what's often referred to as the 'Sandwich Generation'. In this case it refers specifically to women being pulled in every single direction in midlife.

Dr Ben Webb, the brain health expert we met in Chapter 8, explains: "Women experience the three P's: puberty, pregnancy and perimenopause. These have tangible effects on a woman's brain." They also have tangible effects on some women's physical health and well-being. I discussed the implications of the menopause and perimenopause with several podcast guests, who shared their perspectives on how best to navigate this challenging time.

During this phase of life, many women experience 'brain fog' and, depending on the woman's age, this can coincide with when confusion starts to occur. Forgetfulness is usually an early sign of mental decline and dementia, which is a result of brain ageing and not a result of brain fog. However, the similarities between brain fog and age-related mental decline can cause much anxiety, and people worry it could be a sign of dementia. Ben explains there is, unfortunately, no easy test to distinguish between the two situations, but only a very small number of early-onset Alzheimer's disease cases appear around the same time as brain fog. If you are in your 40s or 50s, it's much more likely to be menopausal.

Another incredibly common problem associated with the menopause is disturbed sleep. During the menopause, a woman's brain loses control over their sleep–wake cycles. This is caused by the decline in hormones like oestrogen. To go further, insomnia is often associated with symptoms such as night sweats, depression and thinking disturbances during the night. And it goes without saying that if you're not sleeping well, it's going to affect your mood and your memory. Stress can also exacerbate menopausal symptoms, so managing stress during that time of life is incredibly important too.

Ben suggests hormone replacement therapy (HRT) and menopausal yoga to help your brain health. HRT boosts the hormonal levels that decline during menopause. Women who have used it often find their motivation, energy, focus and memory quickly improve. Menopausal yoga is a holistic approach that some women prefer to trial before being prescribed HRT, which can also have a positive impact on your physical health.

Move it or Lose it!'s Julie Robinson has experience in this area. She experienced an early menopause and found a gap in the market to help other women like her. Realising that women are still not getting the right menopausal support and information to help them live their best lives, Julie founded MenoHealth, a programme that allows people going through the menopause to discuss the challenges they're experiencing and find support to take control of this stage of their life. Sessions are informal and each one focuses on a topic, such as HRT, weight gain, brain fog, osteoporosis – all the things women could be affected by. Men are also very welcome because, as Julie says, "Menopause affects everyone – everyone knows a woman, and that will affect them and their life too."

Menopausal mermaids

Experiencing health issues during the perimenopause, needing a hip replacement and feeling generally lousy, Nicole Morelli decided to do something about it. With a friend, she took the plunge and tried open-water swimming in the Atlantic Ocean. Nicole recalls: "I think we lasted about two minutes, squealing and shouting. But we had such a laugh and when we came out, the buzz was incredible. We were back the next day and the next day and the next, and five minutes turned into 15 minutes."

Based in Portrush in County Antrim, Northern Ireland, Nicole's 'tribe' now has a Facebook group of over 2,200 members at the latest count and approximately 80 members who actively swim. Nicole has organically founded Menopausal Mermaids.

Chapter 9

The benefits of open-water swimming have been widely discussed and debated, but Nicole's experience shows they are endless, not only medically but mentally. A range of women swim with the Menopausal Mermaids: those who are retired, who are grieving or who have depression, anxiety, angina, arthritis and high or low blood pressure and other health conditions. Nicole explains: "Everybody has a reason for wanting to do it. It's really a lifeline for some women. It's just like therapy."

Obviously, there are safety precautions that need to be considered before swimming in the sea, or other open water:

- Check the weather and the conditions of the sea.

- Find a safe place to swim.

- Wear safety floats.

- Swim with others. If you are the only one swimming, make sure there is someone on the beach or bank watching you and take a whistle into the water in case you need to get someone's attention.

There is a lovely social side to Menopausal Mermaids too. After the swim, they always go for coffee and cake, and during the pandemic they even sat in cold baths while on a video call! As we have heard so many times already in this book, the social aspect of exercise and activity is perhaps as important as the activity itself.

If you are wanting to give this a try, follow Nicole's suggestions:

- Find a group that suits you.

- Go with a friend – there is safety in numbers and that way you can't chicken out!

- Invest in the correct gear – hooded towels, a dry bag, a big cocoon jacket – and always take a little bottle of hot water for afterwards to warm your feet and hands up and rinse off the sand.

If you're trying open-water swimming for the first time, Nicole advises: "Get your breathing under control first and don't jump in. Walk in gradually, ease yourself into it and splash a bit of water on your face and around your body. Try to stay in, even for a couple of minutes – it takes your body about 90 seconds to adjust to the cold. After that, it can be quite euphoric."

Living so close to Avon Beach in Mudeford, Dorset, I've seen for myself how popular open-water swimming has become: from those wearing full wetsuits, swimming along the coast, to people in bobble hats and swimsuits who enjoy taking the plunge all year round. I've observed the groups who meet each morning for their regular dip mostly being women of perimenopause and menopause age; they're laughing and chatting with their swim buddies, clearly getting a lot of benefit from not just the cold-water experience but the companionship. Could this help you navigate the challenges of ageing while providing a welcome boost to your mental health and social life? It sounds good to me.

Overcoming indulgence

Menopausal Mermaids use cold-water swimming to help handle life's stresses, which is one way of taking control of our health and well-being into retirement. Other people reach for a glass of wine or a slice of cake, but the truth is that doesn't work long term.

Speaker, author and morris dancer Duncan Bhaskaran Brown knows – he tried it for 20 years. One glass leads to another, one slice leads to another; it all leads to problems.

After two decades of overdoing it, Duncan cleaned up his act and now spends his time helping people push overindulgence out of their life, whether that is related to food, alcohol or scrolling too much on social media. In our conversation Duncan explains that he sees life as a journey on which we're all trying to improve ourselves. He wants to help people move in the right direction, whatever stage of life they're at. "I think it's good to understand the difference between indulgence and overindulgence. I don't want you to never enjoy life ever again."

For Duncan, the problem started with chocolate because "it's a socially acceptable drug for nine year olds". His schooldays were not happy times and his coping mechanisms were based around food. As he got older, his unhealthy habits progressed to smoking and drinking alcohol. Duncan remembers: "I was drinking a couple of bottles of wine a night, and it was so obvious that something needed to change."

Luckily for Duncan, he discovered Allen Carr, the world-renowned smoking cessation expert. When it became obvious that Duncan was drinking too much too, he applied some of what he remembered from Allen's method to help him remove alcohol from his life. Now in his mid-40s, he feels better than he did in his 20s. His mission is to share the energy, focus, peace and freedom he has found to help others transform their own lives.

The tipping point

So, at what point do you say that you are overindulging?

Duncan explains there's no easy answer: "When you talk about alcohol, people just want a number. They want to know if this number of units per week equals having a problem." Duncan believes "you have a problem when you have a problem".

With so many things like food, alcohol, television, gaming, social media or even sporting activities, we start off doing them because we think they help us reduce our stress. But after a while, they actually start to contribute to it and once they stop helping us relax, they become the source of tension. That's the point where you have a problem.

Personally, I'm very aware that when we say yes to something, we're also saying no to something else. If I'm going for a swim, I'm saying no to spending time with my family. If I'm saying yes to playing hockey on a Saturday afternoon, I'm saying no to something else happening in my life at that moment. Everything has a trade-off.

Duncan answers some of my dilemmas. When it comes to choosing how to use our time, he says, "There's quite a big difference between hockey and TikTok, for example. If you really love hockey, what's the most amount of time you can spend playing hockey? There's going to be a physical limit on it. No matter how obsessed you are with it, you can't do it all day. However, you could spend all day vegging out on the sofa and scrolling through TikTok. And in fact, it's designed to make you do it for hours and hours and hours; its whole purpose is to keep your eyes glued to that screen."

This is why breaking our attention away from activities like using social media is so much harder to do. Duncan believes that concentration and attention is a finite resource, and it's one that we really should be guarding. It is precious. If you don't look after your attention, it will go. He advises making sure there are points in your life where you can just focus on whatever you're doing and not get distracted by things pinging for your attention.

Beating overindulgence

If you resonate with Duncan's experience and want to tackle your overindulgence as you head into retirement, what can you do?

- First, Duncan says you need to identify the voice in your head telling you to have the thing you're trying to avoid and give it a name. (Duncan's is called Hank!)

- Next, accept that the voice doesn't make the decisions. One part of your brain is making the suggestion but it's a different part of your brain that controls your decision-making. This is why giving the voice of temptation a name helps distinguish these two different parts.

- Now ask it a question that is relevant to what you are doing. This could be something like, "How is this going to help?" But if you can be more specific to your situation, it will be more powerful. For example, in Duncan's case, his question was, "How will this help me become a father?" The answer is almost always, "It won't."

This process helps the decision-making part of your brain override the suggestive part and can be very effective. In Duncan's words, "You don't have to be perfect tomorrow morning, but if you're slightly better tomorrow morning, you're at least moving in the right direction."

In the right direction for a successful retirement.

Tackling loneliness and isolation

We've heard many wonderful personal stories of retirement life, but it's not rosy for everyone. Many people suffer from isolation and loneliness.

Dame Esther Rantzen has been a household name for many years since first appearing as a presenter and journalist on our TV screens. In 1986, she famously launched Childline – a free, private and confidential service where children can talk about any issues they're dealing with. Childline is now part of the NSPCC and Dame Esther is still involved. More recently, she launched The Silver Line – a 24/7 telephone support service providing information, friendship and advice to older people. I was honoured to interview Dame Esther about her incredible contribution to the lives of the young and the old. At the time of our conversation, The Silver Line had already received more than 2.5 million calls.

The idea for The Silver Line came about when Dame Esther found herself living on her own for the first time in 71 years; she didn't enjoy it. She remembers telling her daughter who, unlike Dame Esther, is rather religious, that she thought God wanted her to move in with her. Fortunately, her daughter laughed. Dame Esther rang her editor at the *Daily Mail*, who agreed she should write about the experience. That column received a huge response from readers and Dame Esther was invited to speak at a conference hosted by a group of charities called Campaign to End Loneliness, which prompted a lightbulb moment.

If a helpline could help children who had problems they didn't know how to solve, it could also help with this loneliness problem. So Dame Esther spoke to the experts at the conference, all of whom agreed she should do it.

The vast majority of The Silver Line's audience are over 55 and living on their own, not talking in depth to anyone else, and some are not talking to anyone at all. Some callers are living with disabilities, which means they really are housebound, looking at the same four walls day after day. Some callers experience loneliness following the loss of a partner or job, or even loss of sight, hearing or mobility. Anything that has served as a prop in your life, once lost, can leave you feeling like you're in a vacuum.

The Silver Line Friends are volunteers trained by the organisation. They don't provide counselling, but they do offer equal, friendly, enjoyable conversations with callers, something they can look forward to. Dame Esther tells me, "It becomes a real friendship, although you will never meet the person you're talking to. But quite often, it's the only conversation people have throughout the week."

Dame Esther says the experience is therapeutic for callers because they know they will talk to the same person next week. It helps push back their horizon a little. In some cases, it gives them the motivation to do something that week so they have something new to talk about. It can be incredibly rewarding for the Friends as well, who are often older people with a little time on their hands, looking to contribute to their community and make a difference. For some, it contributes towards a sense of purpose in retirement.

Finding your mojo

I remember a wonderful story Dame Esther shared with me that happened shortly after the launch of The Silver Line. During the pilot stage, a chap called John spoke to a volunteer called Wilma. John had been a professional ballroom dancer and had just lost his wife, who had also been his ballroom partner. So he had not just lost a wife, he had lost everything in his world. John was really depressed, so much so that he didn't go out. He barely had the motivation to answer the phone, so Wilma would sometimes have to ring several times before he'd answer. As they got to know each other, Wilma told John that she went to line dancing classes. When he asked if she went on her own, she replied, "Absolutely, and if I can, you can!"

So, John began to go to salsa classes and after a year, he started going to his Sunday night ballroom dancing classes again. According to Wilma his mojo has completely returned! His voice is quite different and his attitude is different. Dame Esther explains: "It may be that that would have happened anyway, but I can certainly tell you that the relationship with Wilma gave him that launch pad – that extra boost of inspiration."

Staying connected

Dame Esther gets a lot from her grandchildren. She's not so sure what they get from her (a huge amount of wisdom and lived experience, I'm sure!), but she believes it is so important to stay in touch with them and other people generally. Staying connected is such an important part of maintaining our well-being as we age.

Dame Esther remembers speaking to someone on the helpline over Christmas who was completely isolated. He had spent 40 years at sea, progressing from being an apprentice to a captain. Once he retired, suddenly that close community he'd been working with was no longer around him. Nobody went to see him and as he's disabled, with various ailments, he can't get out. So Dame Esther introduced him to the seafarers in a 'Silver Circle' (groups of people from The Silver Line community who share a common interest), which has enabled him to build a whole new social network.

According to Dame Esther, loneliness is self-fulfilling – people who are lonely think nobody wants to know them, so they don't go out the door. That makes these people difficult to target. To identify lonely people in your community you can simply knock on their door and say hello. If you take that first step, people are often grateful and receptive.

What Dame Esther discovered early on is that there is no silver bullet for loneliness; no one service can entirely solve the problem. Loneliness is multifactorial. A phone call with a volunteer is nice and a face-to-face conversation is very nice, but you need to have a feeling of belonging to someone, somewhere.

Everybody needs good neighbours

If we took more care of our neighbours, we might go some way towards solving the problem of loneliness. One potential solution to better neighbourhood engagement to tackle loneliness is The Big Lunch, created by Sir Tim Smit, designer of the Eden Project. Everyone brings their own food and gets together as a community on a given day. It ran for five years in Dame Esther's neighbourhood and then stopped, because nobody volunteered to continue hosting it.

Dame Esther tells me the voluntary sector charities would collapse without retired people who put in the time, effort and energy. In return, they are rewarded with a greater sense of purpose, as we explored in Chapter 6. She relates: "You're still living a purposeful life. There are still things that are driving you on, yet you feel you need new challenges. Associate yourself with something you think is valuable and important. For me, it's Childline and The Silver Line and a couple of other charities that need me. For other people, it's a football team maybe, or a skill or passion they want to pass on."

companiions

My conversation with Dame Esther reinforced the fact that loneliness is a reality and a huge risk factor as we age. Thankfully, other people like Dame Esther are taking steps to tackle the issue, such as ex-Amazon and Sky executive Lisa Robinson. Lisa founded companiions, an online service that allows people to find support, assistance and company for themselves or their loved ones, helping them stay connected.

It really is an amazing solution for those with elderly parents or family members who they feel might be a little isolated, but are not yet ready for full-on personal or medical care. What they really need is companionship, or someone to do a job or task for them that's become a little too challenging.

Lisa's motivation for setting up companiions was very personal. She found herself struggling to juggle being a parent to young children, looking after her elderly parents and balancing her career without any options to support her as she tried to do her best. Then, when she had to move overseas for her child's health, Lisa realised she had "left a great big hole in her parents' lives". What if something were to happen to them? Lisa started to look at all the care options available and found most were really expensive and inconvenient. So she set up companiions, with the aim of bringing affordable companionship to every community.

Flying the nest

Lisa highlights that people don't live close to their parents as much as they used to. More than ever before, children of elderly people are travelling the world and pursuing careers in different countries – maybe this is something you find with your family; I certainly see this with some of my clients. Yet, despite a greater demand for care facilities, support provisions haven't increased and it's a worldwide issue. There are not enough care agencies and social care services to look after the ageing population that most countries have. Lisa says the problem is only going to get worse. Her view is that a lot of the time people don't need a carer – "they need a kind person to help them do a few things, whether that's fixing their lunch or just conversation, because they feel lonely".

Lisa recalls one of companiion's clients, a 103-year-old war veteran called George. Although George had carers who went in several times a day, it was usually only for half an hour at a time and they were always busy doing their set tasks. George often complained to his son Ashley that he felt very lonely. So Ashley found out about companiions and booked Rob.

In his early 30s and fascinated by the military, Rob loved listening to George's war stories and seeing his medals. They ended up striking up an amazing friendship. During the Covid-19 lockdowns, they would catch up on the phone because they had become such good friends. It was a mutually beneficial and rewarding relationship and made such a difference to the quality of George's later life.

My 95-year-old neighbour, Peggy, who chatted with me for an early podcast episode, visits another elderly neighbour most days. Elsie is 102 and still manages to look after herself in her own home, with her son visiting from some distance away as regularly as he can. She has a weekly visit from a cleaner and a gardener to tend her beautiful garden and if Elsie needs a job doing, Peggy enlists her son or one of the other neighbours to help. I have no doubt that Peggy's companionship and support are invaluable to Elsie maintaining her independence.

Ageing without children

companiions allows children of elderly parents to make sure they are cared for, even if they can't be there in person. However, not everyone in retirement has family members they can turn to for help. There are currently one million people over 65 who don't have children and that figure is expected to double by 2030.

Kirsty Woodard has spent the last 30 years working on issues around ageing, but in more recent years, she has turned her attention to helping those one million over-65s who don't have children to look after them as they age.

Kirsty wants the issue of ageing without children to be more widely acknowledged. The state will generally step in if you get to the point where you can't feed, dress or wash yourself. However, before you reach that point, finding solutions to that everyday, low-level help is much more difficult. Kirsty advocates putting older people in touch with one another so they can provide mutual support, either through corresponding online or meeting face-to-face. Connecting these people allows them to share information about the support that does exist – there is a phenomenal range of services and help available, like companiions, if you know where to look.

Kirsty highlights that when older people are having problems and struggling – for example, if they're having a difficult time in hospital or having issues with their carers – the people who advocate for them and make that struggle known are generally their children. If you don't have anyone to make a fuss to about it, who would know?

So Kirsty came up with Alterkin, a proposal for an alternative next of kin. Using this approach would allow you to set up a circle of support providing social companionship, advice and advocacy, along with practical help. It would also, at an early stage, encourage people to make some plans for later on in their lives.

However, one of the biggest problems people face is that our health and social care systems often make it difficult for people to help if they are not relatives, as we will find out more about later in this book. According to Kirsty, the cultural and policy shifts needed won't happen until we've experienced a change in thinking and what we mean by the word 'family'. If friends, neighbours and communities are going to do more to help the oldest generation, then our systems need to adapt to accommodate this change.

Whatever your family situation, having people in your life who can offer companionship and step in to help if you need is so important as you get older. What can you do to stay connected throughout your retirement and who can you surround yourself with?

How can you take control of your health and well-being?

This chapter has been all about equipping you with the tools you need to keep you feeling better for longer. Health and well-being are multifaceted. Maintaining your physical fitness as you age is important to enable you to do the things you want to do for as long as possible. However, of equal importance, is your mental health. Keeping your mind active and your social network connected are vital components for a happy and healthy retirement. After reading all the experts' insights in this chapter, do you feel better prepared to start taking control of your own health and well-being as you enter retirement?

Key takeaways

- Evidence shows that staying socially connected and keeping active, both physically and mentally, can reduce the risk of age-related illnesses such as dementia, cardiovascular disease and hypertension.

- There is no one-size-fits-all approach to health and well-being in retirement. There are many options you can try and it doesn't have to include going to the gym if that's not for you. From strength training to tai chi to open-water swimming, there is something to suit every personality and individual health need.

- One of the biggest concerns for people approaching retirement is the risk of isolation. Support from family and/or professional or voluntary services can help you stay connected and maintain an active role in society.

If you were to carry out a lifestyle audit, how would you score on the physical, mental and social scales? My neighbour Peggy still does her morning exercise routine every day, which involves the notoriously challenging 'plank', sit-ups and a brisk walk along the beachfront. Walking ensures that Peggy chats with other people each day, which helps her feel connected. She tells me that keeping moving has helped her remain fit and well for so long; Peggy was still water skiing into her 70s!

What changes do you need to make to ensure your retirement is as healthy and happy as possible, for as long as possible?

What barriers are stopping you from making more healthy decisions?

No one knows what the future holds for their health, but now is the time to take control of the wheel of life and give yourself the best chance of living a happy and vibrant retirement.

CHAPTER 10

Accelerator 6 – The Big D

The third and final accelerator for the self-care lever is understanding, living with and preventing dementia, **The Big D**.

It's increasingly common for me to meet with clients in their 60s who have direct experience with dementia. Of the four parents they have as a couple, quite often, one will have lived with dementia. This direct experience creates awareness of the impact it has had on them and their family, making dementia pre-eminent in their thinking. They don't want to experience it themselves and they also don't want to become a burden on their children. Many have made the decision that there is not a chance of them living with dementia and ending up in a residential care home. I've heard everything from, "Push me off the top of a mountain" to "Put me on a plane to Switzerland".

They're all terrified of dementia.

However, as you get closer to the likelihood of it happening to you, and as the probability increases, attitudes tend to shift. Instead of a little bravado or flippant comments about how we might deal with dementia, we seek the support, closeness and comfort that comes from being with family. And, in reality, if there is something going on in our brains and it's happening quickly, we're unlikely to know.

To what extent do you feel equipped to prevent or deal with a dementia diagnosis?

As it progresses, various treatments and therapies are emerging that can have a positive impact. In fact, dementia is one of the big nuts the global medical profession is focused on cracking and a vast amount of research is being undertaken for the medicinal prevention and cure of the disease. Within the last six months while writing this book, two new drugs have been approved by the Food and Drug Administration in the US for the treatment of Alzheimer's disease.

And while dementia remains a disease without cure, there are ways to ease its impact. When dementia happens (and it's not by any means inevitable), we need to understand it and put the right support in place – there's a broader issue at stake here: mental capacity and financial vulnerability. This isn't only about dementia.

The world is moving at such a pace, sometimes it's difficult to know what we need to pay attention to. Take banking, for example. In the past decade or so, the way in which we manage our banking has changed dramatically. Gone are the supportive local branches; the default has become online or app-based banking.

If such changes happen at the same time as our brains are less well-equipped to deal with complexity, confusion is the most likely outcome. The financial services regulator, the Financial Conduct Authority, is rightly banging the drum about consumer vulnerability, not only for financial planners but all financial institutions.

We become less vulnerable when we have specific expertise in a given area. Reading this book will, I hope, arm you with some of that knowledge you need to be less vulnerable, when it counts.

I'm a financial planner, not a doctor or a scientist, which makes the insights from experts in this accelerator especially valuable. In the following pages I explore some of the latest thinking around the condition and what steps you can take to support loved ones living with dementia, protect against mental decline, handle the loss of mental capacity and reduce your risk of a dementia diagnosis.

Preventing or delaying the onset of dementia

We know how feared dementia is and the risk of developing dementia doubles every five years from 65 onwards. Research into our understanding of The Big D has grown exponentially, along with our knowledge of how to have the best chance of preventing it and how to live well with dementia.

Sir Muir Gray, who we first met in Chapter 8, explains that one of the best things you can do to prevent or delay the onset of the disease is to do something challenging. Recent research is changing preconceived ideas about the brain and how it works, as I already touched upon in Chapter 8. Previously, it was thought that as we age, our brain cells die off, but this is not the case: the brain can constantly form new neural connections (known as 'neuroplasticity'), no matter your age.

However, for these new connections to form, your brain needs to be challenged. This can be achieved in part through activities like puzzles, but the biggest results are seen through regular interactions with others and having a sense of purpose. In fact, a lack of connectivity, social engagement, positivity and mental challenges are now recognised as major risk factors for dementia.

According to Sir Muir, as we get older, we get better at making decisions because "you've been making these decisions for many years; you've made mistakes and learned from them". In his book, *Increase Your Brainability—And Reduce Your Risk of Dementia*, Sir Muir outlines three evidence-based strategies to reduce your risk of needing social care or developing dementia and frailty:

1. **Protect your brain tissue**. Sleep well, manage your stress levels and don't take too many drugs (including those prescribed by the medical profession).

2. **Keep your blood flowing.** The second most common cause of dementia after Alzheimer's disease is what's known as vascular dementia, which is caused by reduced blood flow to the brain.

3. **Stay connected.** Socialise in a positive manner. Seek out challenges and opportunities to meet and engage with more people.

Sir Muir says that one of the best ways of challenging your brain and increasing your activity on a physical, cognitive and emotional level is to help other people more: "Helping others is one of the best means of helping yourself."

How can *you* take on board Sir Muir's words of wisdom?

Dealing with a dementia diagnosis

Sir Muir, along with Dr Ben Webb in Chapter 8, has shown us how we can improve our brain health and hopefully delay the onset of dementia or reduce the likelihood of a diagnosis, but what if it does happen? How would you deal with a diagnosis?

Dr Noel Collins, co-author with Mary Jordan of *The 'D' Word: Rethinking Dementia*, is an older-adult psychiatrist whose work relates directly to diagnosing memory problems and delivering appropriate treatment for patients living with dementia.

When we spoke for my podcast, Noel explained that dementia remains a clinical diagnosis and when diagnosing a patient, doctors have to demonstrate that the patient's memory, along with other brain functions, is declining over time to a degree that impacts their day-to-day function. This functional decline cannot be accounted for by something else, such as depression or another medical problem. Noel says, "It can be a tricky diagnosis. It sounds like quite a simple thing to diagnose but it isn't, particularly when there's a context of fear and worry." He explains that ageing isn't purely a biological process – developing wrinkles and our legs giving way – it's influenced by many non-biological factors too, things like social policy, the law, finances and, also, dementia.

Looking at dementia through a more sociological lens and a non-medical lens gives Noel a different perspective when treating his patients. He says, "The biggest risk factor for dementia is age and so, naturally, as our society ages and that life expectancy increases, the prevalence of dementia rises. As each generation is living for longer, medical professionals aren't sure how long our brains are supposed to live for." When discussing a memory problem or a possible diagnosis of dementia with his patients, Noel tries to give a positive outlook on the situation and, in his experience, many people with dementia go on to live very happy and fulfilling lives.

When talking about preventing and living with dementia, it's often intellectual activities that first come to mind, such as Sudoku or crosswords. However, in agreement with Sir Muir, Noel suggests that social and physical activities are far more important, because we humans are social creatures: "We know that loneliness is toxic to our health. What can happen before people develop dementia and, particularly afterwards, is that they become socially isolated and that can become very, very toxic."

For people suffering with memory problems and/or dementia, Noel offers this nugget of wisdom: "Don't be an ostrich; don't put your head in the sand." He explains that, as we get older, almost all of us will be personally affected by dementia in some way – either we will develop the condition ourselves or someone we love will. So why not think about what that means now? Why not think about how you want your care to be? This is the time to consider what you would want. Would you be happy moving into a nursing home if there were risk factors at home, like wandering? Or would you want to stay at home at all costs and accept any risks?

I have these difficult conversations with all my clients as part of their lifetime financial planning. Having the finances in place to support how and where you would want to live if a diagnosis came your way brings enormous peace of mind.

Noel agrees that talking about mortality and dementia throughout our lives makes us much better equipped to deal with it later on. He also urges us to think about the big question of memory and what it actually is. He tells me that we are not defined by our memories and having dementia doesn't take your personhood away from you.

Thankfully, other professionals in this area of medicine are on the same page as Noel and are taking great strides towards shifting not only perceptions but helping people live well with dementia.

Why dementia is not a death sentence

You'll be well aware by now that one of society's biggest fears of growing old is being diagnosed with dementia, but Dr Ben Hicks feels very strongly that a dementia diagnosis is not a death sentence.

Psychology lecturer at Bournemouth University and Deputy Director of the Ageing and Dementia Research Centre, Ben is working hard to challenge and change perceptions and stereotypes of dementia. Using a wide range of disciplines and expertise across the university, he has formed an advisory group to support people living with the condition. This group is constantly consulting a group of older people and people living with dementia to give the lecturers an idea of the areas into which they can expand their research.

And they're doing some groundbreaking work.

Ben was a guest on one of the very first episodes of *The Retirement Café Podcast* and reminded me that dementia is an umbrella term for a range of symptoms. This can include things like short-term or long-term memory loss, communication difficulties and problems with navigation and orientation. Therefore, this term can miss a range of different symptoms. The most prominent underlying condition that causes dementia is Alzheimer's disease, which most people know, but there are other dementias: vascular dementia and Lewy body dementia. They all do different things within the brain and can result in different symptoms, but they all fall under the category of dementia.

Stopping the stigma

There is a lack of understanding around what dementia is and because of this it has very negative connotations. Where 20 years ago, cancer was deeply feared, misunderstood and labelled 'The Big C', the progress made in successfully diagnosing and treating cancer has helped shift public perceptions. Ben hopes the same focus on tackling The Big D will, in time, bring about similar attitudinal shifts towards dementia.

Ben believes it is very possible to live well with dementia: "However, in order to do that, you need to get an early diagnosis so you can access the right support groups, and you also need communities and society to understand it better."

So what is the best way to deal with a diagnosis of dementia?

Ben strongly recommends finding a local support group, which can be found through the Alzheimer's Society. When a diagnosis is made, the burden often falls to a person's partner and it's important they find informal groups to discuss and share experiences too so that it doesn't rest purely on their shoulders.

When running one of his own dementia groups, Ben used gaming technology – iPads, Nintendo Wii and Microsoft Kinect games consoles – to play games such as bowls, tennis and dancing, all of which the people playing had experienced previously in real life. This was a safe way for them to experience their favourite activities while also accessing modern society. Ben believes there's no reason why people living with dementia can't access the same technology everyone else is using. It's one way of challenging stereotypical assumptions.

Ben wants to promote positive living with dementia while supporting people to enact their human rights – the right to lifelong learning, to access activities that are meaningful to them, to provide them with social stimulation and to meet and engage in new groups. He believes the only way to achieve this is to keep challenging public perceptions and create more dementia-friendly communities. Life shouldn't have to stop after a dementia diagnosis.

I wholeheartedly agree, and so does Grace Meadows.

Living well with dementia

Grace Meadows is a trainee musician, music therapist and, at the time of our conversation for the podcast, programme director with the charity Music for Dementia. I was excited to talk to her to understand how music can reconnect those living with dementia to 'normal' life, but also to the people they care about.

According to Grace, no matter what somebody is living with, when you're working with them in music, you still get to see them for who they are, beyond their condition. She explains that music allows her to work using a strengths-based ability model rather than a deficit model, which focuses on what someone is unable to do. Opportunity and potential are boundless with music.

Grace describes music as an incredible tool that enables her to connect with people living with dementia in an encouraging and supportive way. Not only that, it also lets them connect to the world and the people around them and contribute to their communities and families. Music allows individuals with dementia to be in the here and now.

Music for everyone

Many people believe that to reap the benefits of music therapy, you need to be musical. Grace tells me this could not be any further from the truth: "We are all innately musical beings, whether we believe that to be true or not. Whether you think you've got a good singing voice or not, or whether you've never picked up an instrument in your life, everybody has the capacity to be musical and to respond to music because, actually, music is hardwired into us."

For people living with dementia who no longer have verbal capacity, the ability to respond to music is still very much present. Music can aid simple tasks like getting up in the morning or helping someone settle in the evening. It also helps address some of the symptoms of dementia, such as anxiety, depression and apathy. Grace tells me, "When someone has dementia, they can feel really rather unsafe, but music has an emotional resonance for them that makes them feel safe and connected." Music also helps address the care balance as it is a fantastic leveller – partners can be partners and family members can be family members, as opposed to caregivers. Grace suggests making time every day, even just five minutes, to have a musical connection together. This can be through listening to a favourite piece of music that resonates with the person with dementia, encouraging eye contact, communication or hand holding.

Grace concludes: "Dementia is so personal in terms of how it presents and in the way it affects people. We know there's a standard response, but what we also know is that because music is processed across the whole brain and not just in one area, people have these incredible responses to music."

It's widely accepted that one of the implications of a dementia diagnosis is that, over time, you are likely to lose the capacity to make your own decisions. But the loss of mental capacity doesn't only come about as the result of living with dementia; other people can suffer from this too.

The following guests share their insight into the world of mental capacity and how to plan for and deal with a loved one losing theirs.

Assessing mental capacity

Tim Farmer was, as far as we can tell, the first nurse to have evidence accepted by the Court of Protection in a mental capacity case; he changed the face of mental capacity assessments. This led Tim to develop his first business, which set out to provide families with general mental capacity information as well as offering mental capacity assessments. Tim's aim was to shorten the long waiting list for a mental capacity assessment. Since our conversation, Tim has co-founded Comentis, an organisation that helps companies identify and then protect and support the vulnerable through the use of cutting-edge technology.

The first question I ask Tim when we chat for the podcast is, "When might someone consider having an assessment for mental capacity?" He explains that you might consider undertaking an assessment yourself if you're having to make a controversial decision. For example, you may have decided you don't want to include a certain beneficiary in your will and you feel your decision might be challenged at a later date.

"And what should someone expect to happen during an assessment?"

Tim tells me it can be helpful to work with a company that specialises in mental capacity assessments and can meet with someone first to establish whether a full assessment is necessary. They will be looking for several things, the first of which is the person's ability to understand and retain relevant information: "They have to be able to retain it for the length of the decision-making process." They then have to be able to use and apply the information they've been given and if at any point the client starts to struggle with one of those areas, that's when an expert can conclude they've crossed over the line and that a full mental capacity assessment needs to take place.

This can be quite a difficult thing, both to present to people and for people to hear. Tim explains: "An expert in mental capacity will be trying to see if the person is vulnerable – they're protecting them – and trying to ensure their wishes are being met and protected. When we talk about mental capacity, people often think of it as a negative thing, like a life sentence. However, that is not the case as it's possible to regain capacity." As stated in the Mental Capacity Act 2005, mental capacity is time-specific. If you have a urinary infection, for example, it's common to become very confused, and during that confused state you may not be able to remember information. However, once you have recovered, that state is often reversed.

Many people aren't quite sure what to do when they believe a loved one is losing their mental capacity. Tim explains that the first thing you need to narrow down is the specific decision they are struggling with. Is it something related to finance, property or their will? Mental capacity is also decision-specific, which means it can relate to difficulties just making certain decisions, but not all decisions. Once you have recognised the decisions someone is struggling with it's important not only to seek an assessment, but also to approach a solicitor.

The reason that capacity is decision-specific is because of 'the threshold of understanding'. What you need to understand to make a will is very different from what you need to understand when deciding where to live or what you want for breakfast. Quite often, Tim finds that people are able to make decisions about lots of things, but there is just one specific thing they're not able to understand or retain the relevant information for and it is for that decision they lose capacity.

It's also important to understand that just because someone has a diagnosis of dementia, it doesn't automatically mean they can't make a decision. This is because of something called the 'causative nexus', which is a link between any illness or impairment of the mind and your ability to understand, retain and then use information effectively.

Tim tells me about an 89-year-old lady he met who had early-stage dementia. She had £400,000 in the bank, no driving licence and wanted to buy a £350,000 sports car. It could be assumed that she had lost her mental capacity but, as it turned out, the lady had terminal cancer and had been given three months to live. Her only child had wanted that sports car since he was seven. She wanted to buy the car for him, not her. She'd still have £50,000 left, which would be plenty, even if she lived longer than her prognosis. Tim explains: "Even though she had dementia, she was actually perfectly capable of being able to make these decisions and buy the sports car, which she did. And her son was over the moon about it, as you can imagine."

Anyone can assess the mental capacity of those around them. However, as things become more and more complex, and questions come up around what to do with your money or where to live, that's when Tim advises getting specialists involved. When he talks about a specialist, it's not necessarily a GP or consultant psychiatrist; instead, the specialist is the person who has the most experience and knowledge and can do the best job for the person concerned.

When it comes to planning your retirement and living later on in life, what impact could it have if you or a loved one lost mental capacity? And what plans can you put in place? If you're not sure where to start, my guests in the last section of this chapter can offer some help.

Why 'next of kin' isn't enough

Professor Keith Brown, lead of the National Centre for Post-Qualifying Social Work and Professional Practice, joined me on the podcast to share his thoughts and research findings in dealing with mental health and mental capacity in retirement.

There is a widely held misconception about mental capacity, which causes immense undue stress at highly emotional times: many people assume their next of kin can legally speak on their behalf. Unfortunately, the truth is that the term 'next of kin' does not exist in law apart from in the Administration of Estates Act 1925, in relation to intestacy, which means if you die without leaving a will. Keith explains that when it comes to the power to advocate on someone's behalf, 'next of kin' holds no weight in the eyes of the law. Instead, the Mental Capacity Act introduced something called lasting power of attorney (LPA).

LPAs were created so that you can identify who you would want to act on your behalf should you lose capacity or aren't able to give consent yourself.

There are two sorts of LPA: property and financial affairs, and health and welfare.

An LPA for property and financial affairs can be used while you still have mental capacity or you can state that you only want it to come into force if you lose capacity. You do this at the time of registering the legal document.

It can cover things such as:

- buying and selling property
- paying the mortgage
- investing money
- paying bills
- arranging repairs to property.

You appoint one or more attorneys to act on your behalf and you can either restrict the types of decisions your attorney can make or you can let them make all your decisions.

If you're setting up an LPA for financial decisions, your attorney must keep accounts and make sure their money is kept separate from yours. You can ask for regular details of how much is spent and how much money you have. These details can be sent to your solicitor or a family member if you lose mental capacity and offer an extra layer of protection.

A health and welfare LPA covers health and care decisions and can only be used once you have lost mental capacity. Generally, your attorney can make decisions about things such as:

- where you should live
- your medical care
- what you should eat
- who you should have contact with
- what kind of social activities you should take part in.

You can also give special permission for your attorney to make decisions about life-saving treatment. With both types of LPA, you specify anything that is particularly important to you. I know one lady whose LPA states she would like to remain living at home for as long as possible, but if she does need to go into a care home, she'd like a room with a view of the garden and to be taken into the garden to watch the birds every day.

Many people worry about others getting their hands on their money if they hand over financial decision-making, but Keith explains that the benefits far outweigh any risks in this area. He goes so far as to say that everyone 18 or older should consider putting a health and welfare LPA in place – it's not just for older people. The LPA ensures that should the worst happen at any stage of your life – for example, a life-changing car accident – and you can no longer make decisions for yourself, your loved ones can ensure your wishes are met. The alternative is delegating decisions about your care to the medical profession.

He says, "I would also advise you to have a conversation with your loved ones about what you want to happen to you should a difficult situation arise. Don't just write it in your LPA. Let decisions be your own rather than somebody else making that decision on your behalf."

Setting up a lasting power of attorney

You can write your own LPA using the government website at www.gov.uk/power-of-attorney, but sometimes it is worth paying a solicitor to do this for you. There are a number of reasons for this:

1. You can be certain it's been done and registered correctly.

2. They can offer guidance on how your wishes ought to be expressed to ensure they cater for all eventualities and are capable of being carried out.

3. For advice on the different ways attorneys can be authorised to make decisions, including on their own, or jointly with others.

But what happens if you lose mental capacity and have no LPA in place?

Fiona Heald, a solicitor specialising in working with people in later life, explains that the doctors are in charge when it comes to any health decisions in hospital and that most doctors will talk to the family, with decisions made easily in most circumstances. However, that decision-making isn't always straightforward. Doctors have to take into consideration 'best interest', reviewing all options and deciding based on what is best for the person concerned. Keeping people out of pain and living with dignity, if not in a hospital, are all factors to consider.

Fiona explains that, before leaving hospital, the local authority will allocate a social worker. They have the power to make decisions about your welfare in the absence of a health and welfare LPA. She says, "The trouble with local authorities and with doctors is they don't know you. That's why a health and welfare power of attorney is so important – it allows decision-makers to know you; know what you like and how you like to do things."

Keith recalls a story that highlights just how important this is:

PC Paul Griggs was knocked off his motorbike on the way to work. Unfortunately, Paul ended up in hospital on a life support machine. His wife, and mother of his young child, decided she wanted the life support to be switched off. However, despite being his next of kin, legally, she didn't have the power to make that call. Doctors won't switch off life support machines unless they are absolutely convinced there's no chance of a person recovering. So Paul's wife had to go directly to the Court of Protection to ask for the right for life support to be switched off. The process took almost a year before the decision was finally made in her favour.

Financial affairs

When it comes to decisions about property and finance, where there is no LPA in place and you lose mental capacity, someone must apply to the Court of Protection, which will appoint a court-ordered deputy. If you are ill or injured, Fiona likes to wait four weeks to see if you recover sufficiently to not need an attorney to make decisions on your behalf.

A court-ordered deputy has all the powers of an attorney, including the ability to manage your money, buy or sell property, manage your pensions and investments and carry out inheritance tax planning. However, once an application has been made, it currently takes about a year for a deputy to be appointed. During that waiting period, if you have lost mental capacity, you are effectively in a financially frozen state.

As a side note, Fiona urges everyone to have access to their own money: "Have your own little account. Even if everything comes out of the main account, have your own bank account so you can get hold of money for expenses like paying for buses or taxis to get to the hospital." Joint accounts may be frozen if one of you loses mental capacity (although Fiona sees the banks closing accounts less and less these days), until a deputy is appointed by the Court of Protection.

This is why another of my podcast guests, Holly Mieville-Hawkins, a mental capacity specialist, is such an advocate of LPAs. She explains that the court has an agreed order of preference when it comes to appointing a deputy, usually preferring a friend or family member to carry out the role – it makes sense to appoint someone who knows you well. However, if there is nobody suitable, a deputy will be appointed from a list of approved professionals.

Fiona tells me that becoming a deputy isn't particularly easy. It involves a lot of paperwork, dedication and money. "You have to take out a security bond, which means if you are my deputy, and you run off with all my money, the bond can be called in. The insurance company that you took the bond out with will pay back all my money so I'm not left out of pocket." A deputy will also have to open a new bank account, be named as a deputy and be assessed to decide what level of supervision they should be on by a government body called the Office of the Public Guardian. At the time of writing, this costs £100. Deputies also need to keep accounts and produce them annually to the Office of the Public Guardian to say how they have spent the money and what decisions they have made. The annual cost of deputy supervision is currently £320.

When things go wrong

One of the biggest problems Holly sees with LPAs going wrong is when the person afforded the power of attorney uses the money to make gifts – something not permitted under an LPA. Another example is when the attorney feels entitled to the money themselves – after all, they are doing all the hard work looking after the vulnerable person.

When something like this happens, the wrongdoing should be reported to the Office of the Public Guardian, which will then call the attorney to account. If the person who made the complaint is still not happy with the attorney's conduct, they can apply to the court to remove the attorney. This is usually when a professional attorney is appointed to take over.

Writing a will

Holly explains writing a will remains essential, even with LPAs in place, and a badly drafted statutory will application can cause a lot more cost

Chapter 10

and delay than a well-drafted one. The legislation states that to make a valid will, you need to understand the nature and effect of making a will, and broadly understand your assets. If you don't pass that test of mental capacity, your will needs to be a statutory will, made on your behalf. This might sound really scary and complicated, but in practice, it means your will is written by someone the court authorises to do so on your behalf.

Setting up an LPA may feel like a daunting prospect and some people worry about relinquishing control of decisions about their health and finances to someone else. However, Fiona reassures me, "Just because you've done the LPA, it doesn't mean that person or those people have power over you. Even if you did appoint attorneys to make decisions on your behalf if you lost mental capacity, remember that if you're still mentally capable, they can't use it."

Putting your LPAs in place is one of the important steps I encourage everyone I work with to take, if they haven't already done so by the time we meet. I agree with Keith and would go so far as to say LPAs should be mandatory for everyone when they reach 18; one of life's rites of passage into adulthood.

Protecting yourself and loved ones from financial abuse

There's a type of crime for which there is almost no criminal justice.

According to the National Crime Agency, fraudsters stole an estimated £7 billion from over 3.4 million people in the UK in 2017. Fraud and scams are the fastest growing crime area in the UK and notoriously hard to tackle. In fact, experts believe that less than 20% of incidents are reported, so the true scale of the problem may be much bigger.

The sad reality is that the more vulnerable you are, the more likely you are to become a victim. Losing your mental capacity or living with dementia puts you firmly in that camp. If you're suffering from cognitive impairment, fraudsters can scam you week after week without you ever realising.

With police resources limited in this area, there are people striving to support victims of financial crime. One such person is Louise Baxter-Scott, founder and head of the National Trading Standards Scams Team. She's on a mission to empower us to protect ourselves and our loved ones, and stamp on the fraudsters exploiting vulnerable people. In fact, she was awarded an MBE in 2017 for services to protecting vulnerable people from financial abuse.

Have you ever received a fake lottery letter? These letters claim you have won a prize or inheritance, and you need to pay some tax or a small administration fee before receiving the money. Of course, it's a scam and there is no prize. Cowboy letters, text messages or emails tell you there is money on the horizon; you just need to send £20 for your lucky talisman. Or worse, if you don't send £20, you will experience bad luck, such as being the victim of a terror attack. Another (rather terrifying) scam!

Louise tells me there are thousands of consumers responding to these sorts of letters. The criminals are often part of organised crime groups and generally target older people – the average scam victim is 75.

A hidden crime

Louise explains why these crimes can be so difficult to uncover: "It happens in people's homes and they don't talk about it. Many of the scam victims are socially isolated, potentially living on their own, and they may have experienced some sort of cognitive decline. To compound the problem, we are still a society where people don't really talk about money, especially the older generation. As a result of this reluctance to talk about money, criminals target those people who are most likely to keep the approach secret."

Remember Professor Keith Brown from earlier in this chapter? As well as advising the government on mental capacity, adult care and safeguarding, he also leads national research into financial fraud and scams and wrote the national framework for the government across health and social care. Surely he would be the first to spot that a close family member had become a scam victim?

Keith's mother was a northern lady from Lancashire, not shy at sharing with her son how she felt, but at the time of this story, she was in the early stages of dementia. She was worried about her arthritis, so when someone offered her royal jelly and vitamin supplements to improve her symptoms, she agreed to buy some. Keith only discovered the scale of the scam when he went to visit her one day. His mother had five dustbin bags full of clothes sitting outside her wardrobe. He assumed she was having a clear-out, but as these were clothes he often saw her wearing, he started to have a dig around her wardrobe and drawers.

What he discovered horrified him.

In the space of just eight days, scammers had persuaded Keith's mother to spend £2,500 on supplements. She had bought enough vitamin D in one week to have killed everyone in her street!

Now his mother has died, Keith can tell the story of taking the vitamins to his local pharmacy for disposal with a smile. The assistant brought out a tray for him to put the leftover vitamins on. With a wry smile he produced nine bin bags full of his late mother's vitamin D bottles. She had become so confused and as the scale of the scam had grown, she had resorted to storing all the supplements in the loft. Even though he was visiting three to four times a week, the UK's head of national research into financial fraud and scams couldn't protect his mother from becoming a victim. It's something Keith was severely affected by and which drove him to tackle the problem so many vulnerable people are facing. He explains: "As a son, I wasn't always able to protect my mum, but I'm going to do my best to make sure I can protect and help other people."

One of the first victims Louise Baxter-Scott ever dealt with was a chap in his 90s called Len, who lived in an affluent area.

In 2018 the Scams Team received a call from Len, who'd received a letter saying he had won the Spanish lottery. Their advice at the time was to not respond, put it in the bin or shred it. Later, they ran a campaign in East Sussex called Scam Nasty, asking people to drop their scam letters into their local library. The idea was to create an intelligence bank they could feed back to the government. It was then that Len's carer came forward with concerns that he had been responding to this kind of mail.

It became clear that Len was a victim of 'grooming for older people', where the criminals build a relationship of trust and become people's "friends". Len was spending over £600 a month and had unknowingly become part of the criminal network. He was what is known as a 'money mule', moving money in and out of the country for criminals.

These crimes happen because criminals place their victims, like Len, on a 'suckers list', a phrase Louise dislikes. She prefers to use the term 'victim list'. Your data is then sold on to other scammers and fraudsters, so the volume of contact you receive escalates quickly. Louise found the criminals were often achieving a 60–80% return rate when targeting known scam victims. Some of the repeat victims were sending the scammers £20 every day for 10 years.

Len's experience with fraudsters came about because Louise and the team, which was newly established, got to him too late. Only 5% of scam victims will report their experience. In many cases, they don't even realise they are victims – they genuinely believe they are going to win the prize, or they are too ashamed to report being a victim. Louise explains that the cognitive realisation that you've been scammed and lost a lot of money means some people would rather live in denial. If they had managed to reach Len earlier, they could have broken the cycle of victimisation. Reaching these victims early, before they become groomed and entrenched, gives them an opportunity to avoid becoming engaged.

Preventing the crime

Louise explains that her team's main policy centres on prevention: "Our focus is on trying to stop it happening in the first place, which means we will do ourselves out of a job. That's what we'd like to do."

Friends Against Scams, an initiative set up by the National Trading Standards Scams Team, has a strapline: grassroots to grey roots. Its programme includes a 20-minute online learning module or a face-to-face session. Both educate people about the signs that someone in their world is being targeted by criminals trying to defraud them.

So what are the signs to look out for?

- Receiving a huge volume of mail or lots of different types of mail. Of course, there are also text messages and emails to look out for.

- Taking lots of telephone calls and trips to the post office, buying an unusually large number of postage stamps, and talking about friends you don't know and have never heard of before.

- Referring to the criminals as their friends because they phone them all the time and they speak to them regularly.

- Being secretive. Scam victims are told not to trust other people, because they want their winnings.

Could you or someone you know be a victim?

If you are concerned, have a conversation about what has happened. If you think money may have been removed from a bank account, contact your bank in the first instance, to make them aware and stop any additional funds being taken.

Report it and get some advice either from Action Fraud or Citizens Advice.

You can also contact your local Trading Standards to see if they can provide you with additional support. This could include call blockers to prevent scam phone calls and door stickers to warn off cold callers.

I would suggest getting a call blocker for the telephone anyway, which has the added benefit of screening out legitimate callers who may be selling in an illegitimate way. If you receive a call, ask yourself, "Why has someone contacted me? How do they have my personal details?" The more you question, the more resistant you will become to scams. The criminals don't want to work too hard to earn £20. If you stop it from being an easy win, they usually move on quickly.

And if an offer sounds too good to be true, it usually is.

The Big D, mental capacity and you

Dementia and losing mental capacity are things we all probably worry about from time to time. However, as you get older and enter retirement, you might find these concerns crossing your mind more often. We are all likely to experience dementia at some point in our lives, either from a personal diagnosis or through someone we know, but as the people in this chapter have shown, dementia doesn't have to be a death sentence. With the right support, it is possible to live positively and well with dementia.

> ### Key takeaways
>
> - There are many things you can do to prevent and delay the onset of dementia: challenging yourself mentally, managing your blood pressure and staying socially connected have all been shown to reduce the risk of developing the condition.
>
> - It is not only dementia patients who risk losing their mental capacity. This could happen to any of us at any time of our lives. Having LPAs in place ensures the people you choose have the power to make decisions about your health and finances should the worst happen unexpectedly.
>
> - People with dementia and impaired mental capacity are at greater risk of falling victim to scams. Being aware of the signs, staying vigilant and having open conversations about money can help safeguard you and your loved ones from becoming a target.

Let's return to the question I asked at the beginning of this accelerator: to what extent do you feel equipped to prevent or deal with a dementia diagnosis?

What steps do you need to take now to reduce your risk of developing dementia in the future? If something were to happen to your mental capacity, do you have LPAs in place or is this something you need to prioritise?

Chapter 10

Creating a financial plan as you embark on your retirement journey can prove incredibly helpful to those who may be required to take over decision-making for you in the future. They will be able to see a clearly mapped out plan of how you intend to finance your retirement, when and to whom you wish to make gifts or leave a legacy, and how you plan to mitigate any inheritance tax.

This accelerator completes the self-care lever and is a key component in living a fulfilling retirement. If you take on board all the points in this chapter, combined with understanding the science behind living better for longer and taking control of your health and well-being, you'll be on the right track to health and happiness for the long haul.

CHAPTER 11

Accelerator 7 – Planning for a 30-year retirement

Moving on to the planning lever, the first accelerator we explore here is about **planning for a 30-year retirement**.

In my experience, people tend to underestimate how long they are going to live, especially couples. You might think that if you're lucky enough to live to 86, that would be great. But actually, if you're university educated, had a white-collar job, are in reasonably good health and have looked after yourself, suddenly, you're no longer average. As a couple, there's a better-than-average chance of one of you living into your 90s.

I understand this can cause worry when it comes to managing your finances into retirement. You don't know what the stock market performance will look like by your 90s. You don't know if you're going to have enough money to last. When clients initially come to see me, they're often reluctant to spend their money. Even for those with more than enough in the bank and in their pensions and investments, the uncertainty that comes from not knowing how much is enough prevents spending decisions. They know the money can't be easily replaced. As we get older, the option to return to work and earn more money diminishes. When you do finally retire, your wealth becomes an important source of income for the rest of your life, so it's a reasonable fear to have.

What I find fascinating is the psychology around saving and planning for retirement. We all know that we should start saving early; we should make sure we've written a will and put powers of attorney in place, so what's stopping us?

Author of *Alchemy: The Magic of Original Thinking in a World of Mind-Numbing Conformity* and behavioural economics expert Rory Sutherland has a perspective on this. When we spoke for the podcast, he confessed that he didn't really give retirement much thought until he reached his 50s. Rory explains that in the same way advertisers have found that anti-smoking health messages are pretty ineffective for 19 year olds (who perceive the idea of being in their 50s and suffering ill health essentially as a parallel universe), trying to persuade young people to save for their retirement is incredibly difficult. Only when people come into their late-30s at the earliest, do they start worrying about those things. The vast majority of people who seek help from me to plan their retirement are already in their late-50s.

This inability to see and understand what our future self needs is one of the drivers behind creating auto-enrolment pensions in recent years. Rory touches upon another key barrier to saving and planning for retirement – it's not made easy. Rory explains: "At a very simple level, one of the important discoveries of behavioural science – and it sounds trivial, almost silly, but it's nonetheless true – is we seem to have, as a species, an inherent fear of paperwork.

"Not only does the human brain not want to do it because it's difficult, we also don't do it because we think that if it's difficult, it must be a weird thing to do. Because if this were a normal, sane thing to do, that lots of people did, they would have made it much easier." Rory argues we assume that because contributing to a pension, for example, involves a huge amount of paperwork, it must be an incredibly convoluted thing, which is done only rarely.

Rory continues: "What I'm saying is that the government does this bizarre thing: it spends £25 billion a year incentivising you to make pension contributions and yet makes non-scheduled pension contributions an act of extraordinary bureaucratic torture."

He believes the solution is to make the process of contributing to your pension as easy as making a transfer from your current account into your savings account. It could be as simple as adding a 'top up my pension' button to your pension account website or app. What we're then actually doing is creating a social norm so more people will adopt the behaviour.

If you are fortunate enough to be starting early to plan your retirement, then understanding some of these barriers can be helpful. Regardless of where you are now, I know from helping many couples retire successfully that to live the retirement you really want, despite what life throws at you, you need to understand what your wealth can provide for you and your family into retirement and beyond. As lives get longer, the risk of you outliving your money (instead of your money outliving you) becomes greater.

How much do I need? It's the ultimate question we're all asking ourselves. Let me ask you a question:

How confident are you that you have enough money to provide for your desired retirement?

For this accelerator, I explain what to consider when planning for a successful retirement of a possible 30 or more years. We'll look at creating a cash flow forecast and regular planning reviews, along with tax and estate planning, all designed to give you the confidence you can afford the retirement you really want.

Lifetime cash flow forecasting

At retirement, your whole financial life essentially collapses down to one binary question: will your money outlive you, or will you outlive your money?

This question raises two challenges. The first is having enough money to be able to retire comfortably, and the second is having enough money to be able to stay comfortably retired.

To be clear, when I talk about retirement in this context, I'm talking about financial independence and this means something different to each of us, but I am using the term 'retirement' for ease of explaining the concept of no longer needing to earn money to fund your lifestyle.

When it comes to cash flow forecasting, there are three main things to consider:

1. You need to estimate how long you're going to live.

2. You need to understand the impact of inflation on your money.

3. You must calculate – as best you can – what the return on your retirement savings will be and how to get the return you need.

Those things will give you a number – your number – for the amount of money you need to retire comfortably and stay comfortably retired. You'll then be in a good position to answer the essential retirement question of whether you will outlive your money, or your money will outlive you.

First, let's look at longevity. Even if you're not preparing for a three-decade retirement, a three-decade retirement is most likely preparing for you. The average retirement age in the UK is around 62. The average joint life expectancy – the age at which the second person will die for a non-smoking 62-year-old couple – is 92.

Welcome to modern retirement.

Age 92 sits at the top of a bell curve. It's the average life expectancy for the last survivor of a 62-year-old couple retiring today, but the average or mean is just that – an average. If you've been healthy so far and have had the opportunity of living a good life without too many hardships, you may not be that average. You cannot count on having the average two-person retirement and I think you have to at least conceive of the idea that you're going to live longer, possibly to age 100 or older. While that's great news, it means you need to plan for how you will secure an income that will sustain your lifestyle for more than the average 30 years. Longevity is great – if we're living healthier for longer – but you need to plan for longer than ever before, to be sure your money outlives you.

One way to work out how long you are likely to live is to use the life expectancy calculator on the Office for National Statistics website.

Chapter 11

Remember to also estimate how much you think you will need to fund your retirement – will it be the same as your current income or will some costs disappear? Maybe you will have paid off your mortgage, or maybe as you grow older you will want to travel less, so will spend less on holidays. But in your early retirement years, those kinds of costs might go up as you take advantage of having more freedom to travel the world. So try to work out what income you need coming in to meet your expenditure.

So far, that all sounds quite straightforward – you know how much income you need each year and how long you might live, but let's not forget the impact of inflation. Do you know what inflation is today? In November 2022 (the latest figures available in January 2023 as I write this chapter) inflation hit 10.7% – the highest rate in almost 40 years.

The average inflation rate in the past 53 years since I was born has been 5.84%. In the last 20 years, we've had lower rates of inflation, but it's exceptionally high at the moment, and who knows what the future inflation rate will be. For example, in 1975, inflation was soaring at almost 25%, dropping to 15% in 1976, 12% in 1977 and 8% in 1978, before shooting back up to 17% in 1979.

While we'll never know for sure what the rate of inflation will be during your retirement, we need to make an estimate to work out what your number is. One way to do that is to work out what a £100 basket of goods will cost in 30 years' time. Even at a 3% inflation rate, if you take £100 to the supermarket today, in 30 years' time you'll need £248 to buy the same basket of goods.

So there is our second problem.

Whether you're still accumulating your retirement savings or are already spending them, the ravages of inflation will seriously impact what your money will buy in the future. It becomes pretty obvious that you need an increasing income due to inflation, as the real value of your money decreases over time.

We need to maintain your buying power.

This brings us to the conclusion that a fixed income in retirement cannot be the answer. Too many people make the mistake of not factoring the rise in the cost of living into their income needs. Let's say you have worked out that your cost of living will be £20,000 a year in retirement. You may think an income of £30,000 a year will be sufficient, but your cost of living will outpace that income by year 14. You need to have a plan for getting your retirement savings to a level whereby the income they produce can reliably be forecast to go up 2.4 times during your 30-year retirement, to meet your rising income needs. I will explain how to do just that in Chapter 12.

Once you've worked out all of these figures, you need to bring them all together into a forecasting model, which I call a lifetime cash flow, or lifetime financial plan. I use some advanced modelling software, but you could create a spreadsheet if your finances are fairly straightforward. Your financial forecast needs to include all your assets – your savings and investments, your pensions, any inheritance you are expecting – alongside your liabilities, such as outstanding mortgage debt. You then input what you expect your income and expenditure in retirement to be, and the model – based on a number of assumptions around things like inflation and savings and investment returns – will show how long what you've got will last. The benefit of using a specially designed cash flow forecasting model is that I can model different scenarios, from how to take your pensions and retirement savings to fund your retirement tax efficiently (which pension should you draw on first? Should you defer taking your state pension?) to what happens if one of you dies suddenly (which pensions have spousal benefits? What are the death benefits?) or needs to go into care (how will you fund the costs? Can the other partner remain living in the family home?).

The only guarantee with creating a lifetime financial plan is that it will be wrong. Any model is based on assumptions and those assumptions change over time, which is why it's so important to review what's actually happened each year and update your assumptions. What did inflation turn out to be? What impact has new pensions legislation had on your plan? Have there been any changes to income tax or capital gains tax rules? What do you need to do differently as a result?

While a plan will never be 100% accurate, I strongly believe any plan is better than no plan at all.

Chapter 11

I'm a sailor. If I head out of Mudeford harbour and set off across Christchurch Bay, I might not know the exact course to steer my yacht to get to New York, but I've got a bit of a clue. I know I need to generally head west. And just because I know my route will probably pan out quite differently from what I planned, it doesn't mean I wouldn't create a course to follow, or that I wouldn't have an idea of how long it's going to take me, or that I wouldn't have a look at what the prevailing weather forecasts are.

In reality, the weather forecast will become less and less accurate as time goes on, but I can have a good idea of what it's likely to be. I can also work out fairly accurately how far I will travel, how fast I will sail and in which direction I need to steer my yacht to arrive at my final destination. Like a financial plan for retirement, there are a lot of inputs that go into a passage plan. And as with your retirement, the plan needs reviewing and updating regularly. But the starting point is always the plan.

Once your plan is in place, it's fair to say you could take on responsibility for making sure you stay on track. But let me ask you a question: how comfortable are you monitoring changes in regulation and the environment that may impact your financial plan? Where would you position yourself on a scale of 1 to 10, where 1 is *'It feels quite overwhelming'* and 10 is *'I love spending all my time understanding tax and markets'*? The reason many people have trouble staying on track is that unless you answer 10 to that question and you genuinely love keeping on top of changes to the financial rules, it can become paralysing or just too much for you, especially at a time of life when you're ready to spend more time doing the things you've always wanted to. This is because tax rules change, life brings unexpected events and investment returns are unknown. For most couples I deal with, there's one person in the partnership who's keener on looking at the money aspects. Even that person wants the reassurance they are on track.

Just having the information doesn't always allow us to follow through with what's in our best interests. Ask anyone who wants to lose weight what they need to do and they'll tell you they have all the expertise because, more often than not, they've read a million books and they've tried a million diets. They know they should exercise more and eat fewer calories. It's as simple as that. Except that we know it's not. Just because something is simple, doesn't make it easy. It's even more important to have support to make sure you live a truly fulfilling retirement and achieve all those important things you identified before building your lifetime cash flow. So if you have a dream of, say, rowing across the oceans or helping a community somewhere, the energy has to be there to make it happen. It has to feel achievable and you have to be able to dedicate the time and resources to it. And you need someone to support you.

Aside from the money, taking time each year to check in on your plans for retirement and review what you've managed to do so far, what's already planned for the next year and which dreams you're struggling to bring to fruition, is so important. These are all part of an important 'staying on track' conversation to help people reconnect with what's truly urgent and important in their lives. I help rekindle the energy that allows clients to make progress in their retirement and fulfil those plans and dreams, and to ask what could possibly get in the way so they can work through any obstacles and make sure they achieve what they really want to achieve. After all, you may be planning for a 30-year retirement, but those early years, where you're full of vitality, will whizz past unless you live them intentionally.

Robust retirement planning

Very little in life stays the same, and the investment market is no exception. How can we make sure our retirement plans can withstand the future financial uncertainty and changing market conditions?

Abraham Okusanya is a specialist in providing technical solutions for financial planners, like myself, who help people in retirement. He's the founder of the software Timeline, which supports us to help our clients ensure their pots of money last a lifetime. According to Abraham, financial planners should be stress testing their clients' financial plans for some of the worst-case scenarios – it's essential to effective planning. And that's exactly what his software allows us to do.

From my experience and in my role as a retirement planner, investing successfully is a key part of having a successful retirement (something I will delve into in much more detail in Chapter 12). In investing, there is something called a cycle of 'bull and bear' markets. A bull market is when the equity markets continue to rise for an incredibly long period of time. However, as with all good things, they do come to an end, and this is the bear market – when equities or shares decline steeply. When I spoke to Abraham, we were in a bear market. However, a bear market is all part and parcel of the stock market. He tells me, "If you look at the history of the stock market over the last 400 years, not only in this country but in the US and globally, you find this cycle of ups and downs." These are referred to, using industry jargon, as 'sequence of return risk', which is the idea that the order in which you receive investment returns is almost more important than the actual investment returns you receive.

If you experience poor investment returns in the early stage of retirement, this will have a disproportionate impact on the overall outcome. Abraham built his Timeline software to help financial planners run multiple scenarios and build a financial plan that would work, even in the worst of times. He explains why understanding sequence of return risk became so critical for retirement income planning: "The pensions law was changed to ensure people had more freedom with what they did with their money. However, this has led to a move away from a world where the conversation was all about guaranteeing income in retirement to a freedom that comes with greater risk and responsibility."

Abraham goes on to explain his stance on annuities, which provide a guaranteed income for life, versus drawing down on a pension pot. (Because the older generation are living longer, and therefore needing their money to last longer, more people are investing their 'pots' of money to make them last a lifetime.) Financial planners like me need to put a lot more thought into how they help their clients around this shift, using a lot more data. That's why I choose to use Timeline, with the aim of making the forecast as accurate as possible.

Timeline uses 120 years of global market data to help advisers help their clients make these now critical decisions. Abraham reinforces my view on retirement planning: "The future is unknown and unknowable. If we build a plan and we stress test the plan, we can look at the impact of several different bad scenarios that we've known in the last 100 years. If our plan looks like it's going to be okay in those market conditions, then we can proceed with confidence."

As human beings, we cannot make rational decisions when our minds are filled with fear. Abraham has always believed that it is at these times when a financial planner earns their keep, because they can have a conversation with the client and try as much as possible to empathise with the pain and fear they are experiencing and offer some guidance with kindness and compassion.

As an early adopter of Abraham's Timeline software, I have seen the critical difference it can make in helping clients create a robust retirement plan. Not only can it road test your plan against worst-case scenarios, it can also inform and educate what retirement really looks like for your cash flow model and your investment returns. When choosing a financial planner, finding someone who understands the importance of cash flow planning and who goes the extra mile to stress test your plan can give you the peace of mind to confidently take your plan into retirement.

State pension matters

A state pension will form part of any retirement plan, but when it comes to getting yours, do you know how much you'll be given when you retire, or when you'll start receiving it? And is it really so important?

The state pension is a weekly payment from the government that you receive when you reach state pension age and, for some, it plays a vital role in their retirement income planning. It's guaranteed income for life, whereas the shift away from defined benefit pensions and annuities towards pension drawdown plans has reduced the guaranteed element of many retirees' income.

State pension age

The state pension age is reviewed regularly by the government, mainly because, as we know, people are living longer and spending a larger proportion of their adult life in retirement. At the time of writing, in January 2023, the state pension age is 66 for both men and women. However, an increase to age 67 is being phased in from April 2026 to April 2028, depending on your exact date of birth. There's also a further proposal to phase in an increase to age 68, between April 2037 and April 2039.

State pension amount

Once you've started to receive your state pension, the amount you get will increase every year from the beginning of April. In 2010, the government committed to increase the value of the state pension by at least 2.5% every year, until at least 2024. The increase, known as 'triple lock', would be the greater of 2.5%, average earnings growth, and price inflation as measured by the consumer price index (CPI). The government subsequently broke that triple-lock pledge during a bout of irregularly high average earnings (following the Covid-19 pandemic), but we're guaranteed its return from April 2023.

The amount is paid without the deduction of tax but it is classified as taxable income. So, if you have other income streams that take you up to the annual tax-free allowance, you will have to pay some income tax on your state pension. The state pension provides you with a very valuable guaranteed income in retirement, which currently has excellent inflation proofing.

State pension forecast

As part of your retirement planning, I recommend you get a state pension forecast. This can be built into your lifetime cash flow forecast and you may be surprised at its importance. From April 2023, the new state pension will be £203.85 per week for those who reached state pension age on or after 6th April 2016, which works out at £10,600 a year.

The quickest way to get a forecast of how much state pension you can expect is to do it online. Alternatively, you can print off form BR19 and request a forecast by post, or you can phone the Future Pension Centre on 0800 731 0175.

How to request a forecast online

1. Head to the government website at www.gov.uk/check-state-pension, and sign in with your Government Gateway account. If you don't have one yet, you can create a new account and follow the online instructions.

2. Next, you need to go through the automatic two-step verification process, with a code sent in a text message to your mobile phone.

3. Enter your name, National Insurance (NI) number and date of birth. The system then asks for your proof of identity, so you can select a passport and payslip, for example.

4. With those details entered, you'll receive your state pension forecast – the amount you can expect to receive and when it will start to be paid.

There's more information on this page too. The system will tell you your maximum state pension, based on your history and some assumptions. That amount will, hopefully, continue to be linked to price inflation in the future. You're also warned that your state pension isn't guaranteed and the amount is based on your NI payment record. It assumes you will continue paying NI contributions for a number of years (depending on your NI credit history, age and a number of other factors). Use this forecast to check that you've got the correct amount of NI credits. You can find that information in the section about your NI record.

If you think this record is incorrect, you can challenge it. Alternatively, you can pay voluntary contributions to make up for any legitimate gaps in your record. If you're an employee, you can plug any gaps in your NI record by paying what is known as Class 3 National Insurance contributions. This is effectively buying extra years to make up the 35 qualifying years you need in place to receive the maximum new state pension. Usually, you can only pay for gaps in your NI record from the past six years. However, sometimes you can pay for more than six years depending on your age. You have until 5th April of the deadline year to pay a contribution. For example, you have until 5th April 2024 to make up for gaps in the tax year 2017/18.

There are three ways that you can pay Class 3 NI.

Option 1: Pay monthly via direct debit. To do this, you'll need to fill out a form on the www.gov.uk website.

Option 2: Pay quarterly. With this option, you receive a bill in July, October, January and April.

Option 3: Make a one-off payment.

For the final two options you will need to contact HM Revenue & Customs (HMRC).

Demystifying the new state pension

The state pension is a really valuable payment that I make sure all my clients are taking full advantage of – after all, you're entitled to it and it can play a huge role in providing an income throughout retirement. However, changes in rules in 2016, when what's known as the new state pension was introduced, can cause a lot of confusion.

Let me clear things up.

The new state pension was introduced on 6th April 2016 and is widely thought to be a more straightforward system than the old state pension, which was made up of the basic state pension and the additional state pension. The additional part of the state pension has included many different calculations over the years, from the graduated retirement scheme from 1961 to 1975, to the state earnings-related pension scheme (SERPS) from 1978 to 2000. Then there was the option to contract out of SERPS from the late 1980s. Later, SERPS was replaced by the second state pension, or S2P as it was known, which ran from 2002 up until the new state pension was introduced in 2016. No wonder we get confused about our eligibility!

In a nutshell, what you can expect to receive from the old state pension regime depends on many factors, including whether you were employed or self-employed, and contracted in or contracted out. The new state pension is much more straightforward in that there is a flat rate you will receive each week.

One major difference between the old regime and the new state pension is that you must have a minimum of 10 qualifying years to be entitled to the new state pension – that means at least 10 years of valid NI contributions. If you had only one qualifying year of NI contributions in the old regime, you would have been entitled to some of the basic state pension. To qualify for the full new state pension, you need 35 qualifying years, compared to 30 for the old regime, which is quite a significant difference. If you have less than 35 years – either paid or bought years, because sometimes it's possible to top up your NI contributions, as I explained earlier – you will receive a proportion of the full new state pension.

It's important to know that under the old system it was sometimes possible to claim additional state pension based upon somebody else's NI record, but that's generally no longer the case. With the new state pension, your pension benefits will be accrued on your individual records. Having said that, there are transitional provisions to recognise shared or inheritable additional state pension accrued before 6th April 2016 and for certain married or formerly married women who paid reduced-rate NI contributions.

As we've seen, the UK state pension has been subject to many iterations over the past 60 years. Despite these changes, it is something you are entitled to and should remain an important consideration when planning for your retirement.

So where does tax fit into all of this and how can we increase our tax efficiency during retirement? That's what I'm going to look at next!

Minimising lifetime tax

Most people would like to minimise the tax they pay. The clients I deal with are really quite happy to pay the right amount of tax; they just don't want to pay too much. Minimising your lifetime tax is about taking advantage of the opportunities and the allowances available to you throughout your life, not just once you've retired. Everyone's financial position is individual, so this is not advice, of course, but there are some factors you can consider in your retirement planning to make your situation as tax efficient as possible.

Firstly, pensions are very tax advantaged in the UK, so consider whether you can make any further contributions. You need to understand the annual allowance and lifetime allowances, which are the maximum amount of money or investment funds you can contribute or hold in a pension before you suffer further tax charges. This complexity of pensions does offer planning opportunities.

You also have an annual capital gains tax allowance. So if you've made gains (or profits) on property that's not your main residential home, or on shares, we try and utilise that allowance each year so that the amount of capital gains tax you're liable for is minimised. It's also important to understand that you can offset any capital losses you make in any tax year against your gains, which is a key step we take at the end of each tax year for our clients and one you should look to take advantage of too.

It's important to have knowledge of all the different taxes, the associated tax rules and the interplay between them to be able to take advantage of them. And doing so year in, year out, as your circumstances change, will ensure that your overall lifetime tax is as low as possible.

Tax and pensions

When it comes to the tax you pay on your retirement income, one big benefit of pension income (which could be from a defined benefit or final salary pension, an occupational pension, your state pension or your personal pension arrangement) is that it doesn't suffer NI. If you view NI as a tax, which I must admit I do, that's a kind of tax break. The tax nirvana for many higher-rate taxpayers would be to fully utilise your pension contributions during your working life, to receive the full 40% tax relief on your contributions, possibly even more depending on a number of other factors. If you can achieve this as a couple, even better. When you get to that point of financial independence, ensuring you and your spouse or civil partner have a dual income coming in is probably the most tax effective. That's because you can both take advantage of your personal allowances, and maybe even your dividend allowance, depending on the source of your retirement income. It's far more tax efficient for each of you to have an income of £40,000, than for just one of you to be drawing an £80,000 retirement income.

One huge benefit of having a private pension arrangement, rather than a defined benefit or final salary plan, is the ability to pass any remaining funds on to your chosen beneficiaries tax-free upon your death. What an amazing gift to your children or even grandchildren to inherit a pension plan that doesn't suffer inheritance tax! Choosing the best way to draw down on the savings and investments you've acquired over the years is a real consideration that not only impacts the tax efficiency of your retirement income, but the tax efficiency of your estate after you're gone.

The lifetime allowance

If you're in the fortunate position of having accrued pension benefits verging on the lifetime allowance – the maximum amount your combined pension savings can be worth – there are further considerations to avoid incurring an additional tax charge when you withdraw the money. While finalising this handbook, the government announced the lifetime allowance was to be completely abolished, but the details are yet to be fully worked through. This illustrates why pension planning is so complex: the rules are continually changing! This change will have a significant impact upon many higher earners. As the rules stand today, it's important to plan ahead to best predict the value of your pensions, not just when you first plan to draw an income, which is when their value is tested against the lifetime allowance to see whether you've exceeded it. If you decide not to take your pension at that point, it'll be tested against the lifetime allowance again when you reach 75. Depending on the growth you've had in your pension fund in the intervening years, you may face a further tax bill that you weren't expecting. These testing 'events' are called benefit commencement events and there are a number of them, for which an experienced retirement planner will help you plan. However, bear in mind these factors may no longer be a consideration by the time this book is printed!

Should you spend a bit of that pension now to reduce its value? Or should you spend the growth? What's the right call for you? This is where detailed planning with regular reviews becomes critical, to make sure your retirement is planned as tax-efficiently as possible. Planning enables us to answer these questions accurately. In an ideal world, you should start tax planning for your retirement as far ahead as possible, to give you the best chance of making full use of all tax reliefs available. Remember, we're talking about minimising your *lifetime* tax bill, so it's not only about making sure your retirement income is tax efficient, and your estate when you're dead, but why not plan early so you're saving tax-efficiently for retirement?

Tax efficiency once you're retired

As you get closer to retiring, I look at all your income streams for the rest of your life to understand which are taxable and what further taxes might be payable later on. It's all about this lifetime tax.

I was working with someone the other day who owns 26 properties. They are already in retirement and their expenditure is met by defined benefit pensions and state pensions. They've come to the realisation they don't want to run a 26-property portfolio into their 80s and 90s. So I asked key questions: when is the right time to start de-risking yourself and actually reducing the property exposure that you've got? Which ones have made money? Have any made a loss? Can we offset any losses against the gains? It becomes complex.

Working alongside my professional network of tax advisers, I help my clients put some really good tax mitigation strategies in place. The old saying 'tax is taxing' is true if your situation is complex. It's probably not the most exciting of topics, but being efficient with your tax can make a huge difference to your financial future.

Estate, legacy, and inheritance tax planning

Estate planning and legacy planning are terms used interchangeably in retirement planning, but they both relate to planning for your assets upon death. For me, estate planning focuses more on your monetary assets, while legacy planning tends to focus more on the intangible assets. In my opinion, the aim of estate planning is to reduce the burden on your loved ones at the end of your life and after you're gone.

Being brutally honest, how confident are you that you will die organised?

Hopefully, you've got many more years ahead of you yet, but if you had to answer that question, where do you feel you're at? Would you say, "I regularly review my estate planning documents"? Or are you more, "I've got a will but it's out of date"?

In the work I do helping people retire successfully, I work with experts in tax, wills and trusts to make sure my clients' estate planning is up to date, tax efficient and well organised. In short, estate planning is about ensuring your will and any expression of wish are up to date, that you have powers of attorney arranged and any trusts are still relevant or put in place if needed. Ultimately, good estate planning means you're maximising your wealth to provide financial security for you and your family. It allows you to die organised.

Getting started: writing a will

So where should you start when creating an estate plan?

Most professionals would say start with your will. Your will needs to take your lifetime planning into account to reduce the chances of additional tax becoming payable on your death. You don't want your beneficiaries to receive less than was intended, simply because you did not make a suitable will with a solicitor who is capable of understanding and advising on lifetime estate planning.

It's important to know that if you die without a will – known as dying intestate – arranging your assets and affairs will become very complicated for your family. Intestacy rules are incredibly complex because if a suitable beneficiary cannot be found, the government may be entitled to seize the full amount of your assets when you die.

So what makes for a good will?

First, value your estate. Get an idea of what your estate will be worth by drawing up a list of your assets and liabilities. Ideally, you'll have a lifetime cash flow forecast which shows what your estate is likely to be worth on your death, taking account of the need to pay for care fees and other costs that may come your way.

Next, decide how you want to divide up your estate – who will get what. Include details of what should happen if your chosen beneficiaries die before you. If you have children, you need to decide who will look after them if you die before they turn 18. You may also decide to leave a donation to a charity.

A very important step is to choose your executors carefully – who's going to sort out your estate and carry out your wishes after your death? Then, make sure you follow the correct procedures to sign your will, otherwise it might not be valid.

You can write your own will, but there are occasions when you might need legal advice. They include:

- if you share a property with someone who is not your husband, wife or civil partner
- if you want to leave money or property to a dependant who cannot care for themselves
- if you have several family members who may make a claim on your will, for instance a second spouse or children from another marriage
- if your permanent home is outside the UK
- if you have property overseas or if you have a business.

Letter of wishes

Another important estate planning document is a letter of wishes, which normally accompanies your will. It is not legally binding but can guide your executors and trustees to ensure your personal wishes are carried out.

You must take care your letter of wishes does not contain anything that could conflict with your will. The letter can advise on anything but the most common things are:

- who to notify of your death or, in some cases, who not to notify

- listing your main assets, including bank accounts, life insurance policies, expensive items or jewellery and their location, which will help your executors with the probate service. Having said that, these items should also be included in your will as the letter of wishes is not legally binding

- guiding your executors or trustees on how you would like any money managed, or trusts created in your will to be run

- advising guardians on how you would like your children to be raised, their education and where they live

- giving more detailed information to help your executors identify specific items you are giving away in your will

- providing explanations as to why you have excluded someone from the will, if you think that it may be a controversial decision or challenged later.

A letter of wishes can also include what you want to happen at your funeral, whether you want to be buried or cremated and any other specific instructions. Bereavement services specialist and the man widely recognised as the founder of the natural burial movement, Ken West, emphasises the importance of making your funeral wishes known, both formally and informally, to reduce the burden on those you leave behind. When planning a funeral, The Good Funeral Guide website is a helpful place to start.

Whatever you decide to include in it, a letter of wishes should be written in plain English, signed and dated, but not witnessed, to avoid any claim that it has become a legal will.

I discussed the reasons for putting lasting powers of attorney in place in Chapter 10. LPAs were introduced as a replacement for enduring powers of attorney (EPAs) as you can provide more specific guidance on the two different areas (property & finance and health & welfare) and they are registered immediately. If you already have an EPA, this can still be used, but it can only be registered when you've lost mental capacity, which can be more difficult to do.

There's a lot to consider when creating an estate plan, but there are some services that can help. Vicky Wilson is the founder of Settld and she joined me on the podcast to tell me all about her company's service, which is similar to the government's Tell Us Once initiative – a free service that allows you to let all the government services (DVLA, local council, etc.) know that someone has died. Before Settld, there was no such service for the private sector, which informs over 750 private companies for free so you don't have to contact each in turn. That's well worth exploring.

Legacy planning

Legacy planning is about leaving behind a legacy that makes a difference where it matters most to you. Where do you sit with your own legacy planning? Are you confident your executors will have absolute clarity on who should benefit, or is it something you haven't even thought about? Most people are somewhere in between.

Trusts can play an important role in making sure your assets are protected and passed on to your loved ones. There are several different types of trust, which I cannot go into in detail in this book but, suffice to say, trusts can offer a number of tax and other benefits.

Traditionally, trust funds are set up to ring-fence assets for children and young people who aren't yet financially independent. In addition, trusts are a fantastic way to reduce, or even avoid, inheritance tax payments altogether and can also be used to provide advance payments to family members to allow them to receive an inheritance early. If you have life insurance policies in place, diverting benefit payments into a trust is tax efficient. When your life insurance is set up in a trust it cannot be included in any inheritance tax calculation, as payouts on death don't form part of your estate.

Estate and legacy planning are really important parts of financial planning for a successful retirement. Being able to pass on what you've worked for and built over your lifetime is a privilege and something I find clients are passionate about doing. But it needs to be planned for, both in terms of tax and in terms of communication.

A number of my podcast guests have discussed this topic, the difficulties you might come up against, and how to be intentional and successful with your estate and legacy planning. The first I'd like to introduce you to is Kurt Lee, a partner at Lester Aldridge solicitors, who joined me to talk about tax planning and passing on wealth to future generations.

Inheritance tax

It's fair to say that Britain has one of the most complex inheritance systems, making this death duty particularly baffling. Kurt explains there are two elements to inheritance tax: tax applied during your lifetime and the tax paid when someone dies. The amount of inheritance tax payable by someone depends on a variety of factors, including their assets and whether they are married or have children or grandchildren – all these things need to be drawn together and considered in the round.

The inheritance tax you pay in the UK is 40%, but it can be slightly less in certain circumstances. However, broadly speaking, everyone has a nil rate band allowance of £325,000 per person. That's what your estate can be worth before being liable to pay inheritance tax. The government will levy 40% tax on the value of any assets above this level. In addition, you may be able to qualify for the residence nil rate band. Kurt explains that the residence nil rate band is an additional allowance available to those who own their own home and leave it to their lineal descendent – children and grandchildren, with some exceptions – on death. If you decide to leave your residential home to someone else or to charity, the residence nil rate band doesn't apply. It's worth up to £175,000 per person, depending on the value of your home. As Kurt says, "The nil rate band and the residence nil rate band combined are worth up to £500,000 per person and up to £1 million for a married couple in tax relief on death."

Before you get too worried about inheritance tax, keep in mind that most people don't pay it; it currently applies to only around 1 in 20 estates. However, more people have paid inheritance tax over the past 20 years by virtue of property and investment assets rising in price, combined with the nil rate band being frozen at £325,000 since 2009.

This tax break is capped, so if your estate is worth over £2 million on death, the residence nil rate band begins to taper away by £1 for every £2 over the threshold. By the time you reach £2.7m as a married couple, the residence nil rate band has completely disappeared.

If you downsize to a lower-value home, or go into a care home and sell your house, you can still claim the full amount of relief if you have all the necessary paperwork. It's important that you or your attorneys or executors keep any completion statements and evidence needed to prove the sale.

If you have a large amount of wealth, it is important to seek advice on how best to deal with inheritance tax. Getting this right is not only a concern for you, but also for the next generation who are going to inherit the assets. Kurt tells me, "The best tax planning is always to spend it. When you get to a certain age, every pound that you spend, you're almost getting 40% tax relief on it, and it's really only costing you 60p in the pound."

The gift of gifting

Giving at least 10% of your estate to a registered charity in your will currently reduces the inheritance tax rate applicable to the rest of your estate from 40% to 36%. However, if you can afford to do so, giving away money in your lifetime rather than waiting and leaving large sums in your will is incredibly tax efficient. Based on the current tax rules, you are allowed to give cash gifts of up to £3,000 a year – so with forward planning, you could give away a significant amount without having to pay tax. If you choose to give away more than £3,000 per year, the additional amount will potentially be subject to taxation unless you take advantage of one of the following rules.

There are some types of gifts that are exempt from taxation altogether and include gifts between spouses or civil partners, gifts to universities or charities (subject to certain rules), gifts made out of regular surplus income and any gifts given over seven years before your death.

Kurt points out it's really important to plan for these gifts and to keep a detailed record of all the gifts you give, as HMRC can question any gifts they feel don't fall within the rules at the probate stage. The tax rules are incredibly complicated and it is very easy to get something wrong, which is why advice should be taken from a good accountant, a financial planner and, ideally, a tax lawyer. This is even more important if your affairs are not straightforward, for example if you are in a second marriage and there are children on both sides, or perhaps your estate is very valuable. Kurt suggests looking for a chartered tax adviser who understands tax law "because when it comes to giving advice on estate planning, if something goes wrong, and HMRC challenges it, you've got to have someone there who knows the legislation well enough to be able to argue your case".

Back to your will

I believe creating a will is the best place to start with estate and legacy planning. Kurt agrees, but he also points out that a will can be contested after your death if there is a strong enough reason to do so. He worked on a case where the wife had died in the autumn, leaving an estate valued at £1.1 million. According to her will, her estate passed directly to her husband, who sadly died just a month or two later. His estate was then valued at £2.4 million, meaning it wasn't eligible for the full residence nil rate band.

In agreement with all beneficiaries, Kurt executed a deed of variation for the wife's will, passing some of her assets directly to her children. This reduced the value of her husband's estate on death to below £2 million, allowing their executors to claim the full residence nil rate band.

Kurt suggests there are some circumstances in which you need to review your will as part of your estate and inheritance tax plan, such as when:

- you read in your Sunday newspaper that new inheritance tax rules are being introduced. Could they affect you?
- you have a change in family circumstances. When big events in your life take place, for instance getting married (for the first or

subsequent time), having children, getting divorced, cohabitating with somebody else or receiving a life affecting medical diagnosis.

It is incredibly important to get advice about inheritance tax for complex estates. Not only could professional advice save your estate money, it could also save your beneficiaries and your executor a lot of hassle in the event of any issues or disputes after your death, as my next two guests illustrate.

Successful wealth transfer

Within this arena of planning, there is a worldwide phenomenon taking place; different countries call it by different names. In the UK, it's known as 'shirtsleeves to shirtsleeves in three generations'. Japan calls it 'rice patties to rice patties in three generations'. In Italy, the phenomenon is called 'from the stables to the stars and back to the stables in three generations', and in Brazil it's 'rich father, noble son and poor grandson'. Regardless of the name, research by The Williams Group in America suggests that inherited wealth rarely endures. By the second generation, 70% of family fortunes have been depleted and, by the third generation, the figure is 90%.

Lisa Snyder of the Institute for Preparing Heirs in California tells me, "We're very tuned into preparing assets, but nobody's preparing the heirs. So if you think about estate planning, tax planning and financial planning, those are all absolutely fundamental to wealth transfer, but passing wealth and preparing heirs to receive it is also fundamental to successful wealth transfer."

These are the three main reasons why Lisa believes wealth is not surviving across generations:

1. **The money is unexpected.** If you're not having conversations about your wealth with your family, the heirs may not be prepared for it, or know what to do with it. A surprise is not always a good thing.

   Lisa has seen this occur on many occasions, when a family inherits money after their parents have died and one child says, "That's not what I thought was going to happen. I thought that we were all going to share equally. Why did you get more? I thought I was going to be a trustee. Why did Dad choose you to be the trustee?" This speculation tends to lead to litigation in the US, which is how, in many cases, not only the family wealth gets lost but the family unity gets damaged too. Lisa explains how to deal with this situation: "Think of it like a dimmer switch. You can slowly reveal information. You may never get to the actual amounts and you probably won't get to where the lights are completely on, but don't leave them totally in the dark."

2. **The next generation is unprepared.** If our children, or our grandchildren, don't know something's coming, whether they know the actual amount or not, how can they prepare themselves to be able to handle a new financial situation? Lisa believes we need to help younger generations to be good consumers of professional advice.

3. **The purpose of the family wealth is unknown.** If there's no family mission statement, that wealth can get lost. You may be wondering, what is a family mission statement? Or, what is the point of having one? Lisa explains it is a guidepost for your family and for your advisers and for generations to come. Your family mission statement should articulate your core family values so the third, fourth and so-forth generations can understand and live by those values and be able to relate to where the original wealth came from.

Lisa says, "Successful transfer is really about being able to use that wealth to develop lifetime goals and to maintain family unity." When I asked if we should consider disinheriting children from wealth to try and stop the 'shirtsleeves to shirtsleeves' phenomenon, Lisa thinks not: "I don't think that makes sense, but at the same time decide what it is they need and prepare them. I think the better they're prepared, the more they're going to be able to go out and do."

Rory Sutherland, the advertising legend we first met in Chapter 6, argues that you don't want your children to inherit too much money too soon so they can take pride in their own achievements. Let's say your child is working in London and you or your parents leave them a house in the city worth £700,000. Your child is then in the awkward position where almost nothing they do in their career for the first 10 years can make as much difference to their well-being as having that house. I see wealthy clients who admit to having given their children too much too soon and wonder whether they would have strived harder in their younger years.

Challenging conversations

Discussing your inheritance plans with those involved is clearly important but these conversations are not always easy or comfortable. That's where Amy Castoro of The Williams Group comes in. She helps families trust themselves to have some of those difficult conversations around the transfer of wealth.

Former NFL player Rory Williams founded The Williams Group after he witnessed the negative impact wealth was having on his peers and their families. He saw that wealth wasn't necessarily a positive force and, in some cases, it was actually disrupting their lives and family relationships. He learned from research that it wasn't what the families were doing with their wealth – it wasn't trust or estate planning that was breaking down their relationships – it was the family members themselves that were causing the implosions.

Amy explains there are three core drivers of this type of discord, which are very closely aligned to Lisa Snyder's insight:

1. There's a lack of communication and a reluctance to have conversations about money within the family.

2. The next generation is not prepared and their relationship with wealth is challenging. The wealth is running their lives instead of them running the wealth.

3. There's a lack of articulation or alignment within the family values. Not everybody has the same understanding of the purpose of wealth.

Amy tells me, "Families don't necessarily just inherit wealth. They also inherit the ability to have conversations about money and for most of us, that's not a comfortable conversation to have." The breakdown will often happen when the next generation believes they won't be listened to. In this scenario, Amy will steer the conversation towards alignment versus agreement. She says, "Alignment is if one side of the family is deeply committed to the world being a better place and the other side of the family is deeply committed to the world being a better place, but they have different paths to get there. They can respect and actually appreciate the different paths, if they trust that they share the same goal."

Whatever your financial situation, Amy strongly recommends talking openly about inheritance, no matter how hard it can be.

If you're finding this a challenge, Amy says you don't have to dive right in at the deep end. Starting with questions about our values, what is important to us and what we want to pass on to future generations can be a great place to start opening up the conversation. An independent person like me can often help with these conversations.

When estate planning goes wrong

In England and Wales, you can leave your assets to whomever you want. You can leave money to a charity or friends and family. I've already discussed the importance of having a will – the foundation of all good estate and legacy planning. However, there are some caveats when it comes to writing an effective will. As I mentioned earlier, wills can be challenged after death. If you make provision in your will for some people but not others, it can result in claims being made against your estate.

So what steps can you take to prevent that from happening?

When writing your will, you need to ensure it is as watertight as possible. A will can be contested when someone is ill at the time they made it; there might be concerns about their testamentary capacity – the capacity you need to make a valid will in England and Wales, as I discussed in Chapter 10. Wills can be contested on these grounds if someone is in hospital, has been diagnosed with dementia, if their condition has progressed or if they are taking medication that could affect their day-to-day cognitive abilities.

Quite often, family members will tell their solicitor they couldn't hold a conversation with the person making a will, suggesting they lacked this testamentary capacity. This is the ideal time to bring in a specialist to assess your loved one's mental capacity to ensure their will cannot be contested at a later date. In other cases, wills may be challenged due to coercion. I understand this is quite common in families, especially where you have some family members living further afield. Fraud can be involved too. When the person has no idea they are making a will, it is likely to be fraudulent. In some cases, wills are drafted and a signature obtained or forced, as we saw with the infamous Dr Harold Shipman who was convicted of murdering a number of his patients. Shipman was a GP, whose crimes came to light because the daughter of one victim was a solicitor and knew her mother would not have made a will leaving everything to Dr Shipman. Everything started to unravel when the daughter tipped off the police that the will was forged.

Family expectations can also have an impact. In family farms, and indeed many family businesses, the verbal promise that 'one day, all of this will be yours' sets an expectation of inheritance. Again, this stresses the importance of being clear about your legacy planning and having those difficult family conversations early on. As I mentioned, you can leave your assets to whomever you want and, in England and Wales, you can change your mind at any time. Sadly, some people find they have given up their entire working life on a promise that fails to materialise.

The Inheritance Act, or the Inheritance (Provision for Family and Dependants) Act 1975 to give it its full title, allows certain relatives to have a claim against you or anyone financially dependent on you. It's really important that extended families consider provision of not only children and stepchildren, but also what claims could be made in the event they exclude someone.

When someone dies, all their assets are 'crystallised' at that point. Therefore, anything they own, whether it's clothes, a car, their house or a share portfolio, is part of their estate, which then has to be distributed either in line with the terms of their will or (if they haven't got a will) in line with the intestacy rules. Intestacy is a piece of legislation that dictates what happens to your estate in those circumstances. It is usually your executor – the custodian of those assets – who decides how they are to be dealt with during the administration of your estate. Being an executor is quite a big job and people are often appointed lightly, without them realising the serious nature of their responsibilities.

In England, there are no will readings, but anyone can see a will. Once a grant of probate is issued by the probate registry, it is a public document. You can search online to obtain a copy of the will and you can find out who's dealing with an estate and make contact with them. If you have concerns about a will, seek advice on the government website: www.gov.uk/search-will-probate.

If you think something is wrong with an estate of which you are a beneficiary or to which you should have an entitlement, what should you do in the first instance? I suggest seeking out a solicitor who specialises in estate disputes because they can obtain copies of a will file to see what was discussed at the time it was made.

- Learn how to sign your will properly.

- Choose your executors wisely to avoid disputes. Think about who could claim against your estate if you weren't to make provision for them.

- In England and Wales, will writing is completely unregulated. My recommendation is to use a solicitor who is accredited by The Law Society.

- It is so important to document your wishes, because the will itself is a snapshot of your circumstances at one particular time. For example, if it was made 20 years ago, it's not going to reflect your current situation – you might have had more children or grandchildren since then, or married or remarried, all of which could make it easier to challenge.

In some circumstances, having an outdated will is as bad as having no will at all. It really is important to reflect and review as your situation changes and update your will accordingly.

Chapter 11

Planning for your 30-year retirement

As our average life expectancy rises in a world of increasing financial uncertainty, having a robust retirement plan is as important as ever. This chapter outlines some of the key areas you need to consider to ensure you don't outlive your money and can be confident your financial plan will see you through the inevitable ups and downs of the economy and anything else life throws at you. An effective financial plan enables you to enjoy the lifestyle you want throughout your retirement and leave something for your loved ones in your will.

Key takeaways

- Your pension(s) will probably form a key element of your lifetime cash flow forecast. Requesting a state pension forecast and seeking advice from a qualified professional can ensure you are making the most of these benefits, while being as tax efficient as possible.

- Communication is key. Talking about money can be tricky, especially when it comes to inheritance. However, opening up early conversations with your loved ones ensures everyone is prepared and reduces the risk of your will being contested after you die.

- Financial matters relating to retirement and estate planning can be incredibly complex, so make sure you surround yourself with the right people to help you make the right decisions. Seeking professional advice is an essential part of getting your affairs in order and making sure you stay on track with your plan.

I opened this lengthy chapter by asking the question: how confident are you that you've got enough to provide for your desired retirement? As we've explored the implications of living and planning for a 30-year retirement, it's become clear that it's not just about having enough money to live the retirement you want to experience – it's also about making robust plans for after you're gone.

If something were to happen to you, is all your financial and life admin in order? Is your will up to date? Have you written a letter of wishes? Have you had those all-important conversations with your loved ones about what happens to your estate when you die?

There is a lot of help out there to enable you to create a comprehensive financial plan for your retirement. Hopefully this chapter has given you some food for thought and some ideas of how and where to get started. I touched upon the importance of investing for a successful retirement, so we will take a deep dive into what you should consider when it comes to investing for and in your retirement in the next chapter.

CHAPTER 12

Accelerator 8 – The role of investing

The second accelerator for the planning lever is **the role of investing**.

Assuming you've got a purpose and a plan, you now need to consider investing.

But why invest?

Historically, investing in the great companies of the world has proven to be your best chance of exceeding the ravaging impact of price inflation. I discussed this at length in the previous chapter. Remember the discussion around inflation, longevity and investment returns?

To have the best chance of achieving the returns your financial plan requires, I believe the best route for most people is a global, well-diversified portfolio of company shares. However, if your cash flow forecast demonstrates you have enough money, it's worth considering the reasons for investing your money at all. Here are two compelling reasons:

Firstly, I know most people don't like the thought of seeing their money decline in value. Even if you have enough cash to never run out in your lifetime, leaving that money sitting in the bank, declining in real terms each year due to price inflation, can be mentally challenging. To achieve enough money to pay for your retirement, it's likely you've invested money in one form or another. When you've witnessed first-hand the power of investing, you're likely to want to continue with that practice into retirement.

Secondly, thanks to your financial plan, once you've established that you have enough for your retirement, it's time to turn your attention to the next generation. One of my great influences is US writer Nick Murray, who refers to this as creating a 'river of wealth'. By investing money in the great companies of the world, you could help generate excess returns for the next generation.

How confident are you that your investments will meet your family's needs over a possible 30-year retirement?

This accelerator explores the need for investing to fund a longer retirement, what makes for a successful investment strategy and the behavioural challenges of sticking with the plan. After reading this chapter, I hope you will be able to invest with confidence to have the best possible chance of outliving your money.

Investing for the long term

I was delighted to meet Professor Elroy Dimson at the Science of Retirement Conference in early 2019 as I have had his book, *Triumph of the Optimists: 101 Years of Global Investment Returns*, on my bookshelf for many years.

Elroy Dimson is Professor of Finance at Cambridge Judge Business School, and was previously at London Business School. His research focuses on investing for the long term and he has become well known for studies of the investment performance (since 1900) of financial assets in 23 countries.

Chapter 12

Professor Dimson believes your ideal retirement plan will see you spending your last penny on your last day on this planet. However, since you don't know how long you'll live, you need to plan to leave a bequest. This allows you a buffer if you turn out to be far from average. Professor Dimson reiterates the importance of planning for a 30-year retirement and the challenges this brings. As we know, sticking your money in the bank will mean you'll have lower purchasing power when you spend the money than when you saved it. That's because rising prices tend to outpace the interest earned on cash savings. You need to find a better return on your money.

So which types of investments should you consider, and why? Professor Dimson taught investment management for several decades and believes creating and sticking to a long-term plan is best. He explains how the approach you would take as a long-term investor differs from what you would do if you needed to spend some of your money this year or next.

When you plan for retirement, you're thinking, in part, about the people you'd like to give your money to afterwards. You don't want to plan to spend it all by the age of 65 or 70 or 75 (even though that would be ideal) because, who knows? You may live, like Professor Dimson's father did, for 100 years. What's more, some surprises in life are more expensive as you get older. Professor Dimson explains: "Your clothes may be cheaper, you may not get quite such fancy clothing, you may not plan such fancy holidays, but there may be unexpected and undesired expenses. That means you've got to leave quite a lot for the long distant future." Those unexpected and undesired expenses make planning difficult, because leaving money in the bank is a promise of something that has lower purchasing power in the future. This is why Professor Dimson advises investing rather than putting all your money in a deposit account.

No one-size-fits-all

The best way to invest will be different for everyone. By way of illustration, Professor Dimson explains that property might expect to deliver a higher yield for those who are fit and able to maintain the assets. However, renting out a property is complicated, so although there may be higher returns, the older you get, the harder it can be to manage a property.

Your family circumstances matter – for example, if you have a partner or children who can share the maintenance work, then it could be the right route for you, or you might be willing to pay some of the financial rewards to a management company.

So how do you choose what's right for you?

Professor Dimson's focus would be to start with what is relatively simple and doable. His starting point would be marketable securities (meaning shares, bonds and mutual funds) – the assets that can be liquidated in the long distant future.

The cost of investing matters too – I couldn't agree more. Professor Dimson tells me that if you invest expensively and you hold for a long time, those costs start to look quite large compared to the investment that you've put in. He's in favour of eliminating unnecessary risks, so a diversified holding in a moderate-cost strategy is, he believes, the way to go.

When we spoke, interest rates had been very low for an extended period. That appears to be changing at the time of writing this book, but what would low interest rates mean for the future of bond returns? Professor Dimson explains it isn't clear whether interest rates will stand still, go up a bit or go down. But the very dramatic interest-rate declines we've had over the last several decades are behind us, though until the end of 2021 those were profitable for bond investors. Bonds are issued by governments and companies when they want to raise money. By buying a bond, you're giving the issuer a loan, and they agree to pay you back the face value of the loan on a specific date, and to pay you periodic interest payments along the way, usually twice a year. Bonds are considered relatively low-risk investments compared to stocks and shares.

Professor Dimson thinks there is a role for having at least some fixed income investments, like bonds. It helps retirees to budget, as they know with greater clarity what will be coming in, and it provides an effective hedge against adverse moves in equity markets. I ask Professor Dimson if that fixed income/bond market exposure could be replaced in a portfolio with cash. He explains that compared to cash alone, there is usually a bit more reward for investing in bonds. Again, one size doesn't fit all.

Diversifying your investments

There are some opportunities if you're a bit of a 'rate tart' to move your money around from one deposit institution to another when cash looks attractive for modest amounts. By modest amounts, he means no more than is guaranteed under the Financial Services Compensation Scheme for fixed income deposits, which is currently £85,000. A bit of cash management probably sets people's minds at rest for their short- to medium-term spending needs. However, for the longer term, a well-diversified portfolio of equities is still his preferred choice, and that includes stock market diversification.

Stock market diversification involves spreading your money across multiple markets, and you have pretty much free choice for doing so these days. If you want to diversify globally, unit trusts and mutual funds hold thousands of stocks in dozens of countries and make these investments available at a relatively modest cost. I delve deeper into asset allocation later in this chapter.

We also spoke about factor investing and value investing. Benjamin Graham is considered the founding father of these principles back in the 1930s, which he explains in his acclaimed book first published in 1949, *The Intelligent Investor: The Definitive Book on Value Investing*. In simple terms, smaller companies have delivered a higher return over the long term. Professor Dimson explains that factor investing involves weighting certain parts of the stock market that other people don't want to hold, which can make the prices more attractive. In the long run, those stocks can perform better. Does Professor Dimson expect that trend to continue? All other things equal, if you have two companies that do exactly the same thing, but one is small and illiquid, you would rather own the larger, more liquid company. That preference for larger, more liquid companies might push down the price of small companies, allowing the long-term investor to profit. We're profiting from the fact that some investors will pay away a bit of their return in exchange for better liquidity.

Factor investing has also become very popular. Investors buy factor-based products tilted towards value rather than growth, or small-sized companies rather than larger companies. Even stocks with a particular momentum are a type of factor investing. Professor Dimson says you shouldn't plunge into your favourite factor, but a modest tilt can work.

Uncertain times

What about the latest crisis of the day? What should that mean for your investment portfolio?

Professor Dimson offers me a potted history of the 23 countries from where he has data, between 1900 and 2019 (shortly before we spoke for the podcast). When looking at that data, the more traumatic the crisis, the better the investment returns!

If you run forward through time, and you don't use any hindsight or assume any foresight, if you were to buy into stock markets that were experiencing difficulty (for example, a low economic growth rate, a currency that has depreciated, high inflation or anything that indicates that stock prices have declined), then what you find is, in the long term, you have a rockier ride. On the plus side, buying these low-quality stock markets gives you a higher return, so you can successfully follow a strategy of chasing after bad news.

We talk about people who, when they hear bad news, want to avoid investing or, if they've already invested, are so fearful they want to cash in their investments. Although they don't realise it, these people have left it too late. What they needed was a crystal ball! If you know bad news is going to happen in the next time period, by all means, avoid it, but all we know is what's happening today. When we spoke, the crisis of the day was Brexit. If we had known about Brexit in advance, we might have avoided exposure to sterling compared to relatively stronger currencies. But we didn't know. No one knew.

Professor Dimson reiterates my view that you should be investing for the long term. He tells me, "The important thing is time *in* the market, not timing *of* the market." As a financial planner, I'm always looking at investment models and taking comfort in the fact that in most rolling five-year periods, the markets have delivered positive returns. If we allocate cash or fixed interest to cover the first five years of income needs, longer-term money can be allocated to capital markets with confidence.

This approach also seems to have less emotional impact on my clients when we do experience significant market downturns (more about that later). They have the cash in place to provide the income they need, regardless of equity market wobbles. The phone doesn't ring when the stock markets decline; my clients understand the long-term nature of their investments. Professor Dimson maintains that anything that helps investor self-control is important. He tells me people who work with a financial planner to guide them on their investments should stick with that one person unless there is a clear and compelling reason to move. Otherwise, you can move from one financial planner to another, each with a different frame of mind. It's costly to move advisers and having a long-term strategy and sticking to it is more important than having a new long-term strategy every couple of years.

Evidence-based investing

We know we need to be investing for the long term, but how? Where do you start in choosing the right strategy for you?

Evidence-based investing is a good place to begin the conversation. It's about not investing based on your beliefs or your hunches about what might happen to the economy or world – the global situation, climate change and, particularly, the financial markets and economy are all incredibly hard to predict. Instead, evidence-based investors use index tracking funds and invest by simply tracking the performance of the entire market.

My conversation with senior exchange-traded fund analyst and funds product specialist with Bloomberg Eric Balchunas gives a wonderful insight into the history of index funds. In his book, *The Bogle Effect: How John Bogle and Vanguard Turned Wall Street Inside Out and Saved Investors Trillions*, Eric explains investment pioneer John Bogle's radical ideas that led to the creation of a now vast index fund market, driven by fund management giant Vanguard.

Eric firmly credits Bogle with the boom in index funds and the associated lowering of fund management fees and the overall cost of investing. This came about because Vanguard was set up as a mutual, a bit like a coop, paying profits back to its owners who are the investors themselves. Ultimately, Vanguard's unique structure triggered a revolution in the investing market that can still be felt today. With 30 million investors on their platform worldwide, they offer a straightforward and highly cost-effective way for you to invest for, and in, your retirement, if index investing is your preference.

I had another fascinating conversation with a like-minded proponent of evidence-based investing – co-author of *Invest Your Way to Financial Freedom: A Simple Guide to Everything You Need to Know* Robin Powell. He explains: "You're actually harnessing the intellectual power, information and evidence of the whole market. That's thousands and thousands of people, including experts, all over the world. It's like having that giant supercomputer on your side. If you look at the data, very, very few professional fund managers, over meaningful time periods, are actually able to beat that giant computer." Robin explains that one of the advantages of index investing is its pure simplicity. It is not necessarily easy, but it is simple.

However, even with simple investing, there is still an element of risk. But how do we quantify this risk? Robin draws upon financial planner and friend of mine Andy Hart's description of the three types of risk. I particularly like how Andy uses everyday language and views risk from a broader perspective than just the funds you're invested in.

Three types of investment risk

1. **Completely losing all your money** – this could happen on the stock market; the stock markets could go down to zero. If you're in an index fund, the value of that fund could go down to zero, although it's extremely unlikely to happen. Or, if you're invested in Bitcoin, that could easily go down to zero too (as we saw towards the end of 2022).

2. **Inflation** – because we've experienced such high inflation, we know how serious that can be. It's a slow, steady leakage of your financial wealth. If you're not earning more than inflation on your money or on your investments, then you're effectively becoming poorer, not wealthier.

3. **Volatility** – this is the one we most often associate with risk, but it's the one form of risk you really shouldn't worry about. Volatility is just a reflection of people's thoughts today about what companies are going to be earning and what the stock market will be returning in the future. These thoughts may change tomorrow, they might change next week; there's just no way of telling. The best thing is to accept risk as part and parcel of investing and just hang in there for the long term.

Robin tells me, "Humans are amazingly adaptable, and they adapt to change very quickly. When you invest in the stock market via an index fund, you are investing in human enterprise. People will always need to make money to simply clothe themselves, put a roof over their heads, and so on." As an investor, you can benefit.

Cost benefits

One of the huge benefits, and possibly the biggest benefit of index investing, is the cost. It is generally so much cheaper than active management, where fund managers will pick the stocks and shares they expect to outperform. Robin says that many people misunderstand the impact that fees can have over the long term.

In *Invest Your Way to Financial Freedom: A Simple Guide to Everything You Need to Know*, Robin explains it is very easy to buy active funds recommended in the newspapers that do well in the short term, but if you're wanting to create financial freedom for the long term, then they may not be the best investment. Will we hear of those companies in 10 years' time?

I had the privilege of interviewing twice for the podcast, another huge advocate of evidence-based investing, David Jones. When we spoke, David was Vice President and Head of Financial Advisor Services EMEA for Dimensional Fund Advisors, probably the biggest, best-known, most successful evidence-based investment advisers in the world. I'd like to share David's story.

Thirty years ago, when David started out in financial services, he became acutely aware of the prevalence of high fund management costs and investment solutions that let investors down time after time. He started looking at the products and the retirement plans people had and started to project their returns into the future. David was shocked at how the impact of charges would negatively affect people's retirement prospects. Back then, most people used insurance-based retirement plans or pension plans that had very high front-end charges, the extent of which was often concealed from the clients. It was at that moment he realised that what he thought he was doing – serving the best interests of his clients – wasn't being met by the products that were available to use.

David went through a huge transformation. His practice became fee-based and started using products designed to take out the commission element and be as clean as possible to improve his clients' prospects. Despite being among few proponents of this way of thinking at the time, David and his colleague were picked up by the media, appearing in the papers and on TV programmes like *Panorama* and *The Money Programme* that were investigating egregious pension contacts. After many years of campaigning, stakeholder pensions were introduced as a reaction to some of these really high-charging pension contracts. Everything had to be contained within a 1% fee limit.

David thought their work was done but soon realised he hadn't spent much time thinking about the actual investment element of people's retirement. So he started to investigate. What he found was worse in many respects, because people were following investment approaches that would generally let them down over time. As an adviser himself, he'd felt the frustration first-hand after recommending, with the best intentions, pension or fund managers to his clients. However, coming back a year later to review what had gone on, he found himself having to write out an apology: 'Sorry it didn't work out last year the way we thought it would, but here's this year's crop of recommended managers.' The same thing would happen year after year, which is what eventually led David to Dimensional.

The Dimensional approach

Through his own research, David discovered the Dimensional approach, which had come from the academic world, and it opened his eyes to a whole different field of inquiry into the way capital markets work and how this can be put to good use in people's portfolios. He realised many of the things he had been doing up to that point were the cause of his frustrations. From then on, David started thinking about investing in a very different way. Aware of his responsibility as an investment adviser, David spent a year carrying out his due diligence on Dimensional before he said, with confidence, that this looked like the solution he'd been seeking all these years.

David and I chatted at length about why and how Dimensional is different to other asset managers. According to David, Dimensional is an excellent example of evidence-based investing; its investment approach is based on a belief in markets. Rather than attempting to predict the future or outguess others, Dimensional draws information about expected returns from the market itself. In doing so, it leverages the collective knowledge of its millions of buyers and sellers as they set share prices. Dimensional's investment approach is also grounded in economic theory and backed by decades of empirical research. This transparent approach helps provide peace of mind so investors can stick with their plan. David argues that you don't need to pick the next best stocks; you can stick with an academically proven approach to investing instead.

Investments and retirement

I met David when I had just started my advisory business, MFP Wealth Management. I was looking for a different way to invest my clients' retirement savings and I really didn't want to invest their hard-earned savings based on someone's hunch or wish. The good news is you can have a good experience without having to do any forecasting – I believe you just need to be a long-term investor with a truly diversified portfolio.

David tells me, when you're thinking about investing people's money for their retirement, this is a lifetime of their human capital which they can't repay. You can't get those years back. As a result, David explains why, when you're constructing portfolios and investment strategies for people, you need to be very careful that you are doing it on a very sound basis: "I think one of the things that appealed to me when I discovered Dimensional as an adviser was that it explained so many of the frustrations

I'd had in working with conventional asset managers, where they were holding out their skill as 'We can identify superior returns by stock picking or deciding when to be in and out of the market', which rarely seemed to actually happen in reality." David explains that the academic research suggests there's very little persistency in people being able to systematically pick stocks or time markets to their advantage. It's not necessary for a successful investing experience.

But what does it take to have a successful investing experience?

Like mine, David's starting point is to clarify your goals. What are your desired outcomes? This can tell you a lot about how you should invest your money. Next, you need to work out the rate of return you need to realistically achieve your goals. That's where the lifetime cash flow forecast comes in. Then it's about understanding your needs and using those as a guiding principle to understand the nature of the investments you're putting into your portfolio.

For David, the ultimate key is to stay disciplined, stay on track and know that if markets are volatile, that's what you expected ahead of time. It's easy to be influenced by the plethora of information on investing, whether it's from the mainstream media, social media, your brother-in-law or the notorious bloke in the pub! It can seem everyone has an opinion. But stay in your own lane and tune out the noise because your portfolio and your plan are based on your own needs, not other people's. David says, "Generally speaking, those needs are best served by a really good adviser, because they're going to take some of that heavy lifting away. They're going to help you clarify your goals and put in place an appropriate asset allocation, and they're going to help you stay disciplined amid all the noise around investing."

Asset allocation

Both Professor Dimson and David Jones referenced the importance of asset allocation. In my view it cannot be underestimated. Getting the mix of what's in your investment portfolio right for you and your appetite for risk plays a significant role in having a successful investing experience.

Chapter 12

Let's start with the big picture. An asset is anything beneficial you have or have coming to you. For our purpose, it's anything of value in your investment portfolio. After bundling your investable assets into asset classes, we then allocate or assign each asset class a particular role in your portfolio.

To offer up an analogy, allocating your portfolio into different asset classes is similar to storing your clothes according to their roles: instead of just leaving your trousers, shirts and shoes in a big pile in your wardrobe, you sort them out into their functions. You might also go one step further and sort your wardrobe by style so you create ideal outfits for various occasions. For argument's sake, I have some clothes I'll do the gardening in, some clothes for the weekend, clothes for the office and clothes for possibly a wedding or going out somewhere posh. They're hung in different parts of my wardrobe, and the shoes are in some kind of order as well.

Continuing this analogy, asset allocation helps us tailor your portfolio to best suit you, efficiently tilting your investments towards or away from various levels of market risks and expected returns. Your precise allocations are guided by your particular financial goals. And that's it, in simple terms. If you stop reading here, you've already got the basics of asset allocation. Of course, given how much academic brainpower you'll find behind these basics, there is a lot more to it.

Let's take a closer look at asset classes.

At the broadest level, there are four main asset classes:

1. Firstly, you have domestic, developed, international and emerging market versions of equities, which means the same as stocks and shares. Owning stocks and shares is you having ownership of, or a stake in, a business.

2. Another asset class is bonds, also known as fixed income, which is a loan to a business or government.

3. You then have hard or real assets, which can be compared to owning a stake in a tangible object – that could be commercial property, gold, oil or something of that genre.

4. Finally you have cash or cash equivalents – cash just in the building society, the bank or in your pension fund – which is then invested within the bank accounts. If you were a UK investor, a proxy for cash could be a very short one-month duration bond to the UK government.

Just as you can further sort out your wardrobe by style, each broad asset class (except for cash) can be further subdivided based on a set of factors or expected sources of return. For example, stocks and shares can be classified by company size: small companies, mid-sized companies, large cap companies. They can be classified by business metrics, such as value, growth and profitability.

Bonds can be further classified by types; you've got government bonds and corporate bonds, and then there's a credit quality rating that can be applied (high or low) for the term. Bond loans can be for a short, intermediate or long term, with the term relating to when the bonds are repaid. When designing your investment portfolio, we can mix and match all these various factors into a manageable collection of asset classes, for example international small company shares or intermediate government bonds. Generally speaking, the riskier the asset class, the higher return you can expect to earn by investing in it over the long haul.

David Jones agrees. He says equity is likely to be the driver of the returns in the plan, but not everybody has the capacity or the risk tolerance to adopt a 100% equity portfolio and that wouldn't necessarily be appropriate. So, you're going to design the portfolio to deliver its long-term objectives, which are likely to be driven by more equity investment, with the shorter-term needs for liquidity or volatility dampening. This allows you to stay in your seat when things get a bit rough on the seas.

Once we understand asset allocation, we have to implement it. We've got to turn the plan into action. This is where we select fund managers with low costs, who will track our targeted asset classes as accurately as possible. Sometimes a fund tracks a popular index that tracks the asset class; other times asset classes are tracked more directly. Either way, this approach lets us turn a collection of risk/reward building blocks into a tightly constructed portfolio with asset allocations optimised to reflect your individual investment goals and plan.

If the technical detail is your thing, you may ask, who decides which asset classes to use, based on which market factors? To be honest, there's no universal consensus on the one and only correct answer to this complex and ever-evolving equation. As an evidence-based practitioner, I turn to ongoing academic inquiry, professional collaboration with the likes of Dimensional Fund Advisors and my own analysis. My goal is to identify allocations that seem to best explain how to achieve different outcomes with different portfolios. As such, I look for robust results that have been replicated across global markets, been repeated across multiple peer-reviewed academic studies, lasted through various market conditions and have actually worked; not just in theory, but as investable solutions, where real-life trading costs and other frictions apply.

As more data becomes available, we learn more, and sometimes we improve on our past assumptions. Even though the underlying tenets of asset allocation remain our dependable guide, the bottom line is that by employing sensible, evidence-based asset allocations that reflect your unique financial goals (including your timeline and risk tolerance), you should be much better positioned to achieve those goals over time.

Asset allocation also offers a disciplined approach for staying on course towards your own goals through ever volatile markets. Now this is more important than most people realise: where people fall down is getting in and out of investments. They get halfway into something, then they lose confidence, and try something else. Then they lose confidence again and try something else. They're actually better off adopting an investment philosophy and sticking to it.

Hopefully, now that you're a bit more familiar with asset allocation, you will agree that, when properly tailored, it's a fitting strategy for any investor seeking to earn a long-term market return. But let's not assume it's easy to do. Another of my podcast guests, Dr Greg Davies, explains why.

Behavioural finance and bias

Choosing a suitable investment plan and then sticking with it – what makes it so challenging? The topic has come up again and again through my conversations in this chapter, so let's dive deep into the psychology of investing.

Behavioural finance expert Dr Greg Davies PhD defines behavioural finance as "a mixture of economics and psychology. It is using an understanding of human psychology mixed with an understanding of economic decision-making to try and study how, and why, people make the decisions they do."

Greg is Head of Behavioural Finance at fintech company Oxford Risk. He joined me to share his knowledge and experience of the behaviours behind investing and (most importantly) what you can do to try and change those behaviours to improve your investment experience for a successful retirement.

The problem with decisions

Greg tells me that much of today's younger generation close their eyes to retirement planning. Setting up a pension doesn't sit high on their priority lists and it's only when someone experiences a significant life event – like having a child, getting married, the death of a parent – that they start to think about it. Auto-enrolment pensions are a good way to begin a pension fund: their introduction has resulted in an increase in workplace pension participation from 46.5% in 2012 to 79.4% in 2021 (according to the DWP). Rory Sutherland, who we've met in previous chapters, believes auto-enrolment has been more successful than even the government expected because we feel safe having the same pension as all our colleagues. He likens this to herding behaviour of antelope in the wild: "The reason antelope graze together is so they don't have to spend 50% of their time looking out for lions. If there is a lion nearby, chances are they'll tell from the behaviour of another antelope, rather than by actually spotting it. The same rings true for auto-enrolment pensions. If my pension provider suddenly starts beefing up the charges, I may not notice. If 100 of my colleagues have the same pension, some switched-on person in the finance department will probably notice, and they'll alert the rest of us."

However, from a psychological perspective, they do have their limitations, as Greg explains: "The minute you automatically enrol someone into something, firstly, they automatically get the default option which, by definition, is approximately wrong for everybody. The other problem with automatic enrolment is it gives people the sense that someone else has solved the problem for them, leaving them to feel that they don't have to worry about it." This causes a knock-on consequence – an invitation for people to disengage even further from their finances, and they can disengage right up until they turn 60 to 65. When they get to the point of retirement, they realise they don't have enough money, because their 'pot' has been ignored for the last 40 years. Different ways need to be found to re-engage people before they turn 55.

Greg suggests making things visceral and tangible as this will focus people far more. He explains: "When someone receives a large sum of money, whether that be from inheritance, a lottery win or redundancy, deciding what is appropriate to do with that money, even in the simplest financial situation, is actually a fiendishly complicated decision." If they were to be given a £10,000 lump sum, most people would step away and stick their heads in the sand because they're scared of the complexity of making all the choices around what to do with it. It will end up sitting in a bag, or in a current account, or worse, just spent. Greg believes advisers need to build more tools to help people decide what to do with their money, and this includes looking at the whole situation: "Discussions need to be had about their goals and aspirations and they need to be given a few of the better options to use their £10,000."

Helping people make these complex decisions (or sometimes what might even appear to us as simple decisions) is where I find I can add most value with my clients. It's about being a steady hand to guide you through the decision-making journey that is retirement.

At Oxford Risk, Greg has developed tools to help people make better human decisions. Some of the financial decisions you have to make don't have an answer dictated by the numbers, for example whether you use £10,000 to pay back your sister-in-law after a loan or you put that money into a pension.

The correct answer comes from what's important to you, as a human.

Why the defaults don't work

Greg tells me, "People don't buy numbers, people buy stories and people buy narratives. For every single financial decision that we make, there's a default – there is the decision that people feel very comfortable with if they don't know what else to do; that is, what they default to." Unfortunately, in financial decision-making, the defaults are often very expensive. When people do get over those defaults, the things they have chosen are almost never the ones that have the theoretically 'perfect' numerical trade-offs in them. Instead, they're the ones that resonate with us emotionally and the ones we feel comfortable with.

I would go as far to say that the vast majority of our decisions are emotional decisions. We may think we're making a rational choice, but it's generally our emotions driving our actions. This is why we are all more comfortable investing in things that are suggested by friends at a dinner party – this may not be the best investment in the world, but because you can justify to yourself the reasons why you're doing so, it becomes a good idea.

So what should we be doing when it comes to investing?

Greg shares his three rules to investing, to be followed in order:

Rule one: put your wealth to work and don't leave it sitting in a current account; do something with it.

Rule two: don't put all your money into one thing. Diversify, ideally as broadly as you can. Diversification is the one thing that you can do to protect yourself against calamitous downturns. Another tick in the diversification box.

Rule three: leave your money alone.

These three simple rules fall into the category of things that are simple, but not easy. Yet, as humans, we fail to do them systematically.

Greg says, "If you could genuinely do those three things as an investor, you will do better than 80–85% of all other investors. The reason why we fail to abide by those three rules is because all those three rules are, in their own way, emotionally uncomfortable things to do."

Investing feels uncomfortable because it's moving your money from somewhere safe to somewhere you perceive as risky. However, as we've seen, you need that risk in the long term because it's actually riskier to leave it sitting in cash doing nothing for 30 years. Diversification is emotionally uncomfortable. Why? Because people don't like buying things they don't know about, or don't have a personal story for, when left to their own devices they aren't buying diversified portfolios of good investments. Instead, as Greg tells me, "They buy concentrated portfolios of nice stories, and those are two very different things." Greg believes one of the best things you can do, once invested, is leave your money alone, even when you see the market going up and down and it's emotionally stressful. He explains: "It is uncomfortable, and we feel that we should be doing something, whereas in reality, most of the time, we should be doing nothing. Put your money to work into a diversified global tracker and leave it alone."

The amount of risk that is right for you depends to a large extent on where you are in your life and this comes back to making sure you have the correct asset allocation. For example, if you've just retired and are pulling money from your portfolio that needs to be used for everyday living, then you need to take less risk, because if the market was to suffer a big drop at this time, it could have significant long-term consequences for the value of your portfolio. Whereas, if you are 30 years before retirement, you can afford to take more risks.

Behavioural bias

Behavioural bias is another factor that impacts the decisions we make. I was pleased to have Neil Bage, a specialist in behaviours that drive our decisions and co-founder of Shaping Wealth, join me on the podcast. He explains the main behavioural biases and how they impact our decision-making, particularly when it comes to retirement planning and investing.

Neil tells me, "We make decisions that we genuinely believe will serve our interests and are aligned to our values and our guiding principles. However, when we get bombarded with information, that information can distort our reality without us realising it has been distorted."

There is a behavioural bias called framing. This is when a decision is based on how information is presented to you, as opposed to the underlying facts or the full picture. For example, a group can be asked the exact same question but in two different formats:

1. Do you think you could retire on 70% of your current income?

2. Do you think you could retire on a 30% reduction in your income?

Although it is, in reality, the same question, the way we subconsciously process the information is different, because one is framed in a positive manner and one is framed in a negative manner. We have a tendency as humans to focus more on the negative than we do the positive.

This processing is then released in the form of a decision that was made without us being fully aware that we've allowed the way the information was presented to infiltrate into the end result. We are making decisions based on what we believe to be true, valid and reasonable, without realising these unconscious processes are interfering with the way that we see the world.

Neil explains: "Framing is just one of hundreds of behavioural biases, but it is used a lot to impact our decision-making. A great example is how, during the height of the pandemic, the news was focused purely on Covid-19. Depending on where you got your news from, it was often framed in a certain way, depending on the reporter's angle. If we just accepted all those stories as fact, we could have ended up making lots of decisions based on misinformation." It's why Neil's only sources of information were the UK government, the World Health Organization and anybody who was giving factual evidence-based information. Social media was full of framed noise, and it was highly emotive. Recognising this bias, I took a similar approach and decided to only follow 'Covid for Actuaries' and a number of scientists on Twitter for information about the pandemic.

There are two further types of behavioural bias: cognitive bias, where we make errors in the way we process information, and affective bias, which is where we make a decision driven and affected by our emotions.

Neil tells me, "There are far more affective biases than there are cognitive biases because our emotions are such a dominant part of who we are. Therefore, we have to accept that our emotional state will impact how we make decisions. It's why I'm a big believer in the phrase, 'sleep on it'. This allows you the time to hit the reset button, cognitively speaking."

Neil suggests two skills that anyone can use when making big decisions:

1. **Write things down.** It is very simple, but very effective. This can be in the form of a journal, writing how you are feeling and describing the events that are taking place and how they are impacting you. You can then refer back to passages and try to work out what happened emotionally at that particular point in time.

2. **Have a trusted adviser.** This doesn't necessarily mean a financial adviser; it is someone who you trust implicitly to be able to share your innermost thoughts with and someone who you can reach out to when you are not okay, knowing they will not judge you.

According to Neil, "We need to be really careful that we aren't making decisions that can have an impact on our long-term financial well-being, based on something that we just *think* is right; they should be based on something we *know* is right, because that's where we get into a place of making decisions that will have the right impact on us."

Investing in your retirement

Throughout our lives, we face many complex decisions around what to do with our money. However, as you approach retirement and your ability to make more money reduces, making the right decisions about how to manage your wealth becomes even more important. From investment strategy to behavioural science, this accelerator has given you some expert insights into how to ensure you have a successful investing experience, in a way that suits you and your family's needs.

> **Key takeaways**
>
> - There is no one-size-fits-all approach to investing. However, long-term investing is widely thought to deliver the best returns for those who want financial freedom. Beyond that, the right path for you is dependent on your personal circumstances. A financial planner can help you plan an investment strategy that works for your individual goals and appetite for risk.
>
> - No one can predict what will happen to the stock markets in the future but diversifying your portfolio, seeking advice from qualified professionals and taking an evidence-based approach can give you the best chance of receiving positive returns on your long-term investments.
>
> - In turbulent market conditions, while it can be tempting to move your money around and even change advisers, this is likely to do more harm than good. If you have a robust plan in the first place, sticking with your strategy is the best way to ride the wave of temporary uncertainty.
>
> - Being aware of how behavioural biases may be influencing your decisions will put you a step ahead of most investors on the road to a successful investment experience and a successful retirement.

Investing is complex, but it doesn't have to be. Working with someone you trust to guide you in creating an investment plan that's aligned to your goals for retirement will help simplify the process and give you the best chance of delivering what you need.

The decisions you have to make heading into retirement can be significant. Remaining confident you've made the right decisions is even tougher. I work with some really smart people who are very knowledgeable about investing and about money. What they appreciate from our relationship is sharing the load of responsibility and having someone with sound judgement to offer sage advice, especially when the going gets bumpy.

For the vast majority of people, investing is a fundamental part of having a successful retirement. Following the views of the experts I've introduced you to in this chapter should help you get off on the right foot.

Planning

CHAPTER 13

Accelerator 9 – Care and the end of life

The third accelerator for the planning lever, and the final accelerator of my framework, is **care and the end of life**.

There's a certain inevitability about needing some type of assistance when we get older. That might not involve going into a residential care home, but even support in your own home requires careful consideration and planning.

How do you go about preparing a plan for when you need care later on in life?

The worst thing you can do is wait until you actually need it. There's value in knowing how the care system works and who you would call should you need this level of support at some point.

Most people I speak with don't want to become a burden on their children as they age. As we saw in Chapter 9, modern life increasingly means families are geographically distant, but even those living close by are likely to have busy lives.

The UK care system is complex and challenging to navigate. This becomes even more difficult as the need to plan for care often comes at a particularly emotional time. Having a plan in place for choosing the kind of care you or a family member may need and determining how to fund it can relieve an often stressful situation.

How confident do you feel about navigating the care system and dealing with the final phase of life?

This accelerator explores the fundamentals of how the UK care system works, how health and social care is funded and where to go for further help. It will also look at the final phase of life – how to plan for and deal with death. This knowledge will help you deal emotionally and practically when the time comes.

Navigating the care system

My friend and client, Katrina Moss, experienced a transition into semi-retirement that was far from gentle. I wanted to share Katrina's story in this chapter for reasons I hope will become apparent as you read on.

Six years before we met, Katrina moved to the New Forest from Surrey, after living in her home for over 30 years. Her husband had retired a few years earlier and the move was a form of semi-retirement, but one which turned out to be much more stressful than she could have anticipated. It took the best part of a year to get over the stress of the move, and not long after, Katrina's mum was diagnosed with terminal cancer.

When her mum went into hospital, the standard of care was mixed. Katrina explains: "Some staff were fantastic, caring and very good at their job, while others were verging on negligent. I think if my sister and I hadn't been there, she would have died in the hospital because she needed people to speak up for her, and to let them know what was going on because she wasn't able to make herself clearly understood." They managed to get their mum into a lovely hospice, where she improved so much she was able to move to a care home. Knowing her mum was happy made a huge difference but she still had the emotional toll of knowing her last parent was dying.

Looking after a loved one and providing end-of-life care can be an enormous strain, both emotionally and financially. Paying for care is thought to be the second biggest financial commitment that we make during our lifetime, after taking out a mortgage. Navigating the care market can be a minefield, which adds to the financial pressure people feel.

Jacqueline Berry set up My Care Consultant to help people understand and navigate the UK care system, find the services they need, secure available funding and, importantly, ensure the long-term security of their loved ones. She and her team work with specialists and qualified retirement financial advisers to get the best possible outcome for you and your family members, as you steer a course through the care market. I think this is a phenomenal service and one I recommend to so many people who get in touch with me looking for help planning for care.

Jacqueline and I have spoken a couple of times for the podcast. In our first conversation, Jacqueline explained the difference between social care and healthcare, who's responsible for each type of funding and how to find the most suitable care provider. In our second meeting, she shared her tips on how to apply successfully for the elusive (free) NHS continuing healthcare.

Jacqueline likens the care system to a maze: "So many people seem to be scrambling around from one source to another, desperately trying to find correct answers and information, for themselves or on behalf of a loved one. So it's really important that people get access to the help they need." If you think you or one of your family need to find your way through the care system and are not sure where to start, have a look at how Jacqueline breaks down the initial assessment process:

1. Your local authority (i.e. whoever you pay your council tax to) is responsible for helping you access the care you need; however, seeking practical help from your local authority is optional for those who can self-fund their care. After you contact them, they will arrange a care 'needs' assessment (usually within 28 days, unless it's urgent).

2. A social worker will usually come and see you for a face-to-face needs assessment and Jacqueline recommends a family member also attends so they can input into the assessment. The assessor will look at your day-to-day needs and how they would best be met.

3. If you have 'eligible' care needs, you'll receive a care plan, outlining their recommendation and information on who to contact, e.g. care providers.

4. Finally, they will look at who will pay for the care, which is where a financial assessment comes in.

So how's your care going to be funded?

Most people will contribute something towards their care, regardless of how much they have in savings. If you have above £23,250 in assessable capital/savings, you will be responsible for paying for your social care fees in full. If you have less than £23,250 (current upper capital threshold in England at the time of writing), a local authority will then look at your income. If you're living at home, you're allowed to keep some of your income to pay for things like food and bills. The rest of your income may well go towards your care fees, depending on the level of care needed. But who pays if there's a shortfall? You? The local authority? A combination of the two? The NHS?

When we spoke for the podcast, behavioural economist Rory Sutherland shared an interesting idea to address the country's challenge of how we fund care for everyone – a voluntary inheritance tax, which would pay for certain things such as guaranteed care for the rest of your life. He explains one way in which this could work: "You could simply add an extra year on to the end of your mortgage so you continue paying your mortgage at the same rate for one year extra. That would then buy you, let's say, several hundred thousand pounds worth of insurance in the event that you need care at home."

As things stand, the question of who funds your care can be a complex one and this is why it's important at this stage to establish whether your need is of a social care nature or a healthcare nature which, again, confuses many people.

Jacqueline explains the differences between these two concepts:

Much confusion exists surrounding the funding of care for those in later life. At the root of this confusion is often the distinction between social and healthcare. Despite the many challenges facing the NHS today, it retains responsibility for delivering free healthcare at the point of need if there is a 'primary' heath need, irrespective of the financial circumstances of the recipient. Social care, on the other hand, is the responsibility of local authorities and is means tested.

The difference between the two is not always clear and this leads to much confusion. Securing free NHS-funded healthcare is by no means straightforward and some who should be eligible for this support don't receive it. Eligibility criteria are complex and inexact, the information available is often confusing and hard to find and attainment and delivery is fraught with inconsistencies. At the same time, social care is being cut back and some welfare benefits restricted, making legitimate access to NHS Continuing Health Care provision increasingly important.

Social care

While there is no formal definition of 'social care', it is often described as dealing with the "activities of daily living". In other words, help that is needed in order to carry out day-to-day activities like eating, washing, dressing, mobility and using the toilet. It also refers to help needed to maintain independence, social interaction, manage complex relationships and to be protected in vulnerable situations.

Social care is the remit of the local authorities and is, and always has been, means tested. People often don't realise that social care is not free. The likelihood of needing it is quite high and the cost can be quite high too.

Healthcare

In contrast, a healthcare need is one related to the treatment, control or prevention of a disease, illness, injury or disability and the after care of someone with these conditions. While not defined in law, this definition of healthcare needs is set out in what is known as the 'National framework for NHS continuing healthcare and NHS-funded nursing care'.

At this point, it's important to note that in the case of a dementia diagnosis, it doesn't necessarily follow that you will have substantial care needs – particularly in the early stages of the disease. The side-effects you experience as a result of the condition and the subsequent level of skill required to provide your care will be considered when it comes to deciding the support and funding you're entitled to, not the condition itself.

NHS continuing healthcare and NHS-funded nursing care

There is a third term often relevant to later life needs: funded nursing care (FNC). FNC is a weekly payment made by the NHS to those who a) aren't deemed eligible for full (free) NHS continuing healthcare but, who b), do have healthcare requirements. Importantly, **an individual must be living in a care home registered to provide nursing care** in order to receive this funding, so it's worth checking if the home of your choice is registered to provide nursing care, otherwise you will have to forfeit the funding.

The individual in need of care being assessed (or their legal representative/s if relevant) will be informed if they are eligible for this funding as a result of the same assessment for (free) NHS continuing healthcare.

There are two stages to the assessment process, as follows:

Stage 1 – The 'Checklist' screening tool

Stage 2 – Decision Support Tool assessment

You can ask your social worker or GP to arrange a Checklist assessment for you. You can also contact your integrated care board (ICB) directly to request a Checklist if you are experiencing any problems. Like local authorities, there are many ICBs across England, and they are responsible for administering assessments and funding for NHS continuing healthcare in the local area. If you are unsure of your ICB, you can locate it here: www.nhs.uk/nhs-services/find-your-local-integrated-care-board.

(Free) NHS continuing healthcare is a fully funded package – the full monty in the world of care funding. Jacqueline recommends that anybody being discharged from hospital with relatively complex needs asks for a continuing healthcare assessment if this isn't triggered automatically.

The Checklist

The first stage of the assessment is a fairly straightforward checklist assessment, a screening tool aimed at determining whether you should progress to a full assessment. It can be completed by a number of different professionals if they have the correct qualification, including a social worker, nurse or GP.

The Decision Support Tool

The second stage is the full assessment conducted by a multidisciplinary team using a measurement tool called the Decision Support Tool (DST), which will typically last a couple of hours. The multidisciplinary team is usually a group of three individuals; often two will be clinicians who specialise in different areas, for example a specialist in dementia or cognitive-related illnesses or a cardiac specialist. The idea is to get a broad view of the qualifying criteria from different clinical perspectives to make sure the decision is as fair as possible. The third person is usually a social worker, or possibly a nurse or care home manager.

The process looks at a number of different healthcare categories – officially referred to as domains – and each individual will be assessed based on their level of need in each of those domains. For example, one domain is mobility, so that part of the assessment would look at whether or not you have mobility challenges and how extensive or complex they are.

At the end of the assessment, the team will make a recommendation, which is given to the integrated care board, who will decide whether you are eligible for the funding or not. The good news is, even if you're waiting months for a second-stage assessment, any funding you do receive is then backdated to, at the latest, the 29th day from the date of your first-stage Checklist assessment.

A lady came to see me seeking advice about her brother's pension, because he had become very poorly in his 50s and was being cared for by his mum. She wondered whether there was any way of accessing his pension early due to his ill health. The first question I asked was whether he had been assessed for (free) NHS continuing healthcare. It turned out he hadn't, so she asked the social worker, who confirmed her brother could indeed be assessed for (free) NHS continuing healthcare.

Several weeks later, he was awarded (free) NHS continuing healthcare and a back payment was made, negating the need to access his pension early. The right care was put in place and this gentleman's mother was relieved of the stress of caring for her son.

Part of the work My Care Consultant gets involved in is helping people to prepare for the assessment and therefore giving them the best chance of achieving a fair outcome first time. Jacqueline's team can advise on the sorts of questions you might be asked and help you make sure all the documents you might need, for example care plans and hospital discharge plans, are up to date and available.

Other factors that can contribute towards a fair outcome include asking for some commentary from care providers around their observations of your loved one in the recent weeks, because there can often be quite drastic changes that the assessment team won't necessarily pick up on through documents alone, and that input can make all the difference.

What happens if you're told you are not eligible?

Jacqueline explains that if you don't believe this is the right outcome, there are services available to help you appeal the decision and ask for a reassessment. My Care Consultant can help by explaining the process of how to contest a decision and signposting clients to third-party specialists – for example, legal advice – if they feel that's appropriate. It's also important to understand that (free) NHS continuing healthcare, even if it is awarded, is not necessarily permanent. If you recover from a condition and no longer have complex health needs, then you will no longer qualify for the funding package.

Planning for care

Most people don't plan for care. They don't want to think about it. Many behavioural studies tell us this is part of human nature and I find this is often the case with my clients. It can be a difficult conversation to have, but one that's crucial if you want to be sure you can afford the kind of care you really want in later life.

For me, it's not just about the money side of things. Planning ahead is also about finding a place you'd be happy living if the time arose that you could no longer cope at home. Do you want to have access to a garden? Or lots of organised activities? Do you want to be close to your children so they can visit more often? Or stay in the community you know and love? These are big decisions, but facing up to the reality of what later life may be like can reduce the anxiety it can cause.

What I believe people need is everything pieced together with a clear route forward. It's not just about the situation you're in now from a care and funding perspective, but what happens if your needs change, if your partner's needs change, if you move out of your house, if your partner moves out of your house? How would these things impact you? And what is the financial impact on you if your hard-earned savings are swallowed up by care fees?

Just like financial and legal advice, My Care Consultant sits outside of the local authorities, NHS care provision and professional services, and can help you take a step back and plan that route forward from within a safe space. They will ask you about your individual needs and wishes and provide you with a personalised plan to take forward, including signposting you to the relevant third-party specialist at the right time. They act as a continual touchpoint and confidential listening ear throughout your care journey, so if you have questions along the way, you always have someone you can come back to.

Choosing the right care provider isn't just a financial decision; there's a huge emotional element. It can be an upsetting and stressful time with mixed emotions and even guilt, because decisions are often being made on behalf of a loved one. This is why it's really important you get access to good-quality information and guidance at a time like this.

Funding care

If you or your loved one haven't been assessed as eligible for (free) NHS continuing healthcare, it is likely you'll be faced with having to pay for at least some of your own care. From my experience, people's biggest concern is how best to manage their money to make sure it meets a lifetime of care costs and wishing to leave a legacy for younger loved ones, while often still supporting a partner living independently at home.

You might be asking yourself whether a care annuity is a good idea, or if you should sell the house. Making financial decisions on someone else's behalf isn't easy. If you already have a lifetime cash flow for your retirement, building in the cost of care is fairly straightforward. If you don't yet have a plan, maybe now's the time to find a financial planner, who will gather together all the financial information about the person who needs care, including their income and expenditure, details of assets (like their house, savings, investments, etc.) and their projected care costs for the future. This is the starting point – putting together a full financial picture so you can start looking at funding options.

A cash flow forecast will show how long the money will last and highlight if there's any shortfall that needs to be met. It's a good idea at this stage to request care annuity quotes so you can see the impact it might have on your money. A care annuity, like a pension annuity, is where you pay a lump sum to an insurance company to guarantee a lifetime of care.

I recommended a care annuity to a client of mine called George, over a decade ago now. He was suffering from multiple sclerosis and type 1 diabetes and was only expected to live for a few years. Due to his limited life expectancy, the care annuity costs were affordable. My client's wife and his family have been forever grateful for my advice because George survived for an incredible nine years and the family never had to worry about the cost of his care. They were able to enjoy the extra years George was with them, safe in the knowledge he wouldn't have to move to a cheaper care home when the money ran out.

A care annuity isn't the right solution for everyone, so you should explore other options for paying for care, which may include using savings or investments, or renting out or selling the house. Including your annuity quotes as part of your cash flow modelling will enable you to understand affordability and what impact paying for care will have on the money left over for beneficiaries after death. Importantly, doing so will enable you to accurately compare all care funding options against each other from an informed standpoint.

A care annuity can only be arranged by a qualified financial adviser, and one who offers transparent fees and is independent of any annuity providers should be able to negotiate the best deal for you.

The government website has a host of information about the point at which you become fully or partly responsible for paying your own care fees, so it's a good place to start your research.

End of life

We may not like to think too much about what our care needs might be in the future but, as we've seen, they are an integral part of a successful retirement plan. Another area people often put off planning for is end of life. It can be one of the hardest things to discuss as we get older. How do you even begin the conversation with loved ones?

This is something Judy Kauffmann, an end-of-life doula and bereavement counsellor, sees a lot. She feels passionately that the best way to have a peaceful end of life is to prepare for it.

When it comes to broaching what can be a difficult subject, Judy suggests something as simple as making reference to an article or a podcast so it doesn't become personal. Rather than asking the stark question, "What would you like to happen when you die?", framing it as an interesting topic of conversation can help you approach it in a gentle and non-direct way.

Judy tells me, "When people haven't made their wishes clear, and the family is more or less divided, it often ends in conflict because each individual family member genuinely believes they know what that parent wanted, and sadly sometimes this rift lasts forever." Judy's words echo those of Amy Castoro from Chapter 11 and reinforce the importance of writing a letter of wishes.

Many guests I've had the privilege to interview have stressed how the end of life can be so incredibly hard for all involved. It is not only difficult dealing with hearing the diagnosis for the individual, but also arduous for those who are going to be left behind.

Judy co-authored *End of Life: The Essential Guide for Carers* with Mary Jordan who also joined me on the podcast to explain there are several important points to be aware of when someone is coming to the end of their life.

1. If you are caring for someone at the end of life, tie up loose ends with them. By doing this, the individual gets peace of mind.

2. Be led by the person who's dying. If you do have those brave conversations, you might be amazed by some of the things you're told.

3. No matter what your feelings and beliefs are about death, it's what the individual at the end of life feels and their beliefs that matter.

Speaking about the unspeakable

Judy has found that sometimes family members won't allow their loved ones who are at the end of their life to talk about dying, but she believes it is so important to give them the time and space to do so. It's a process she can help with as a doula. Plugging the gap between the family and the medical profession, her role is to listen to the person and let them speak their truth. Judy explains: "An end-of-life companion or doula can be employed at any stage of end of life, from diagnosis right up to death."

Another of my podcast guests, Sue Barsky Reid, has another approach to encourage conversations about end of life. She agrees the topic of death has a stigma of being too morbid to mention, never mind discuss! However, thousands of groups in 51 countries have met up with one another to talk about our finite lives and the inevitable. This is all thanks to a truly groundbreaking idea that Sue's son, John Underwood, had: Death Cafe.

John was a devout Buddhist, and part of being a Buddhist is recognising and contemplating death. Realising that this is what he wanted to do with his life, to share his thoughts with like-minded people, he and Sue held the first Death Cafe in John's home in 2011. Since then, there have been 15,266 Death Cafes worldwide.

So what is Death Cafe? It is a non-profit social franchise with no formal agenda; people are allowed to talk freely about death. The joy of a Death Cafe is that you don't go to one unless you choose to. Therefore, the people who attend have an interest in thinking about death and dying and there's an acceptance among the rest of the group. Because of this, the discussions that take place during a Death Cafe session are wide ranging – from people sharing their experiences of watching people die, to individuals who want to discuss their death with their children but their children won't listen. Members find it refreshing to come and talk openly with others and have frank conversations with those who work in the death industry.

Sue says, "Some of the conversations are really, really profound and interesting, sometimes sad and often very funny. It sounds like a paradox, but people laugh a lot at Death Cafes." They also enjoy tea and cake as this is an affirmation of life. The analogy is thinking about death while keeping yourself alive and in a pleasurable way because it's cake, not bread and butter!

Sadly, John died unexpectedly. Sue shares his ethos: "You never know when it's going to be the last time that you hug your child. So you need to make sure that you appreciate every moment and live for now. The point of a Death Cafe is to make the most of your finite life. The realisation and acceptance that we're all going to die should help us to be able to live a full life."

Making your end-of-life wishes known

How can you be sure that when you reach your end of life, your wishes will be carried out?

Sarah Malik is a specialist information and support nurse at Compassion in Dying, a national charity supporting people to plan ahead for their end of life. Like many aspects of healthcare, there's no one-size-fits-all approach. People have very different and personal values, and Sarah believes it's very important to allow people to have an end of life in line with their values and beliefs.

In her role, Sarah focuses on bringing real compassion to death. One of the main services the charity offers is creating an advance decision, which is a legally binding 'refusal of treatment' form. It is a statement of instructions about what medical and healthcare treatment you want to refuse in the future, should you lose the capacity to make these decisions. For example, you could use it to say you do not wish to be resuscitated if you develop certain medical conditions. An advance decision often works alongside a health and welfare LPA document, making it crystal clear to your loved ones what care you do and don't want to accept for certain medical conditions in the future.

Sarah shares the story of one caller who was seeking help to put his advance decision in place. Through his mother's illness, he had been opened up to the world of dementia and the sorts of things that can go wrong as the condition progresses. Towards the latter stages of her illness, she had lost the ability to swallow and the medical team was proposing to tube feed her. Having witnessed the process, this chap decided that if he were to ever have dementia, he wouldn't want to have his life prolonged in this way. He chose to refuse all life-sustaining treatment if he were to end up in a similar situation.

Documenting the little but important things

The key to creating end-of-life documents, like an advance decision, is making sure your attorneys – the people who will make sure the wishes you record in your advance decision and any LPA you have – fully understand what you want, and why. These legally binding documents give them authority and they shouldn't be afraid to use it, should the need arise.

Sarah explains there's a second document you may want to put in place as part of your end-of-life planning: an 'advance statement'. It isn't legally binding, but it's a really helpful document because it allows you to outline anything that's important to you in relation to your health and your values and your well-being. It sits alongside your other documents and can help people look after you better.

Some people might write that they'd rather be cared for in a hospice at the end of life. Your attorneys can then try to make that happen. You might want to include that you've been a vegetarian for 20 years, so if you lose the ability to share that with others, at least that's documented. You may have religious beliefs, or it could be as simple as you'd like to have a room with a garden view and be taken out for fresh air as often as possible. These might feel like small things, but they can become really important points that add further context to what you've written in your advance decision.

These two documents together are really powerful for maintaining your quality of life and incredibly helpful for clinicians treating or caring for you. Sarah explains that putting this paperwork in place is all about empowering you to remain independent, even when you've lost mental or physical capacity.

Once written and signed, Sarah suggests creating copies of your documents and sharing them with friends and family, keeping a copy alongside your LPA, and maybe giving a copy to your GP, so it's easily found if the need arises.

Sarah empathises that starting the conversation with your loved ones can feel hard. She found talking about it with her own grandparents difficult, so they took it bit by bit. Sarah says, "The whole conversation doesn't need to be had in one sitting; maybe just broach the subject then let your family sit with it for a while." Compassion in Dying also has a downloadable booklet called 'Starting the Conversation' on their website. You can create an advance decision and advance statement from the age of 18, so with free templates downloadable from the Compassion in Dying website, or from www.mydecisions.org.uk, there's nothing stopping you!

Dealing with grief

At the age of just 25 years old, Amy Florian had the unthinkable happen: her husband was killed in a car accident and she was left as a single parent to their seven-month-old child. Amy's world, dreams and identity were all shattered in an instant. She'd grown up in a small rural town in America where no one knew how to respond to her situation.

Amy tells me, "Of course everyone wanted to help; they just didn't know how to do it appropriately. I experienced unhelpful phrases such as 'Oh, I'm so sorry for your loss', 'God has His reasons', 'Don't worry, you're young, you can marry again', 'Oh, he's in a better place now' or 'Oh, Amy, he wouldn't want you to cry'."

Amy decided she wanted to use her experience to inform and help others in grieving and dealing with death. She went back to education, retrained and is now a Fellow in Thanatology and founder of Corgenius, a company that teaches professionals how to support their clients in times of grief, loss and transition.

Amy explains that the way people deal with illness, death and grieving has changed over time. In today's society we are taught to suppress it, ignore it and deny it. The word 'died' is often replaced with 'passed away', 'six feet under', 'dearly departed' and 'gone to rest'. She tells me, "One hundred years ago, people were exposed to death and dealt with it in a matter-of-fact way. Families cared for their loved ones who were sick, or who were older, or who were dying, and children were exposed to it. It was accepted as a natural, normal, expected part of life." However, as modern technology has increased lifespans and people have started to live further afield from one another, people seem less able to take care of their own family members. Amy believes these developments are not necessarily bad things; they are all good and they're all necessary, but we have to face the fact that these changes effectively outsource death. As a result, death and grief have become scary unknowns that we avoid talking about, making it difficult to understand our experiences or to find effective support when we or someone we love is going through a transition or loss.

Amy draws on her personal experience, education and experience of working with more than 2,000 grieving people to offer some insights into the reality of widowhood and how to help: "When that person dies, every breath the survivor takes all through the day is different: from the time they wake up and reach across to that empty pillow, go down and have coffee for one, bake some scones and have no one to eat them with or see something in the newspaper but be unable to share it. We have to unlearn the expected presence of the other. It is those times when we would expect them to be there. Those are the hardest to let go of, and it takes a very long time to do that."

What is Amy's advice for dealing with grief?

"Don't stuff it down. Allow the tears; there are physiological chemicals in tears that relieve stress. It's part of our stress relief mechanism." She explains that the first year is the hardest. In that first year, there's a lot of letting go but often not a great deal of building anything new. It takes time to know who you are without that person and what your purpose in life now is. However, over time, things will change. "There will be little moments where you catch yourself smiling, or you're able to enjoy something or you laugh. Sometimes people feel they're being disloyal to the person who died if they allow themselves to laugh or smile, but that's not disloyalty at all. Those things are what sustain us through the really dark times."

Amy reminds us: "If someone you know is grieving, don't go away in the second year either, because that time is hard in a different way. That's when the reality truly sinks in that the beloved person is not coming back, and although the griever has done a lot of letting go, they haven't built their new life yet, so it still feels uncertain and emotional. At the same time, all the support has disappeared because everyone assumes that by the first anniversary they're healed. They aren't. They still need your companionship and support, so be there for them."

Healing after death

Amy was determined to heal after the death of her husband. One of the things she did was face grief head on. She went to places they used to go to, but she went alone. She did things they used to do, but by herself. Amy would say the words to herself, "John died; he's not coming back." She read everything she could get her hands on and sought out people who understood grief. However, she found that sometimes all you need is somebody to just listen or sit with you.

If you know someone who is experiencing grief, how can you help them?

Amy says, "First of all, lose all that unhelpful language that our society has taught us and instead learn how to ask good questions. That's so much more important than telling the grieving person something about yourself or what you think they ought to be doing."

She also emphasises that it's not your job to try and fix things: "Your job is also not to cheer them up. Your job is to be a companion to them wherever they are. So be truly present, be there for them and invite them to tell their story. You could ask questions like, what do you hope people remember about them? What did you learn from them? What was really special or valuable about their wisdom and their life?"

According to Amy, one of the biggest misconceptions about grief is that it is only triggered by the death of a beloved person. Actually, grief is triggered whenever there's a break in attachment; whenever you have to leave behind someone or something you like about your life, you're familiar with it, or you're attached to it, and you have to go forward without it, that triggers grief. This can be a person who dies, certainly, but it can also be the distancing of a relationship you cherish, a divorce, leaving a role you enjoy, losing an ability to do something, a dream or a plan for the future, your trust in a societal institution, a shattering of long-held beliefs about how life works (or should work). Actually, even positive transitions trigger grief. A retiree, for instance, has to leave behind their status, their role in the business and the world, their reason for getting out of bed in the morning, the colleagues they associated with daily, and more. The principles of supporting people through all of life's transitions are the same principles used to support them through death, so learning good grief support skills is essential in life and business.

Chapter 13

Death, loss, transition and, therefore, grief are inevitable in life. When they happen, the reality can be extremely painful. Amy offers some final words of hope and wisdom: "Eventually, if you keep doing the hard work of grief, things that at first bring tears can bring smiles. The times of sadness and crying become less frequent and less intense, while the time of contentment or even joy become more frequent and more intense. The sadness and crying never totally go away; people get 'ambushed' for the rest of their lives. But that's a good thing, because it means we don't forget. The point of healing is not to forget. You take that person or experience with you for the rest of your life. You take their life with you. You take their love with you; that never dies. You carry who you have become because that person or experience shaped you, and you remember them always. As you do this, joy is possible, healing is possible. You can't see it right away, but you can get there."

Planning your care and end of life

Talking about care and the final phase of life is a difficult subject for most of us. But deciding on what you want to happen when you need care and at the end of your life is the final piece of the retirement planning puzzle. This accelerator has raised some key questions around the types of care and funding available, how to make your wishes known and dealing with death and grief – questions I hope you feel better prepared to answer as you start to think about your own needs and those of your loved ones as you get older.

> **Key takeaways**
>
> - The level of state-funded care you receive will depend on your level of need and your financial situation. To access gold-plated NHS continuing healthcare funding, you will need to request an assessment by your local clinical commissioning group via your GP or local authority.
>
> - Make sure your wishes are known. From a medical and care perspective, an advance decision document allows you to make decisions about your medical treatment that could

> affect you later, including resuscitation instructions. This best sits alongside your health and welfare LPA and can be supplemented with an advance statement, which explains your personal values, your preferences and how you would like to be looked after.
>
> - Talking about your care and end of life may not feel easy but these conversations are an important part of planning in retirement and crucial for a peaceful end of life. Opening up the discussion with your loved ones is the best first step. If you'd like to talk to someone objective, organisations like Compassion in Dying or your nearest Death Café can help.

Have you thought about what you want to happen if/when you need care and at your end of life?

Do your loved ones know your wishes, should something happen to you? If you have older family members, do you know what their wishes are?

Very few people find talking about their ultimate demise easy, but by planning ahead you really can reduce the burden on your loved ones. Reach out to professionals to help you plan for this final leg of your journey – both in advance and at the time. That's what we're all here for. Why not make the very final stage of your retirement as successful as the preceding 30 years?

CHAPTER 14

What will you do now?

Imagine working through each of the nine accelerators for a successful retirement and how you will feel to have each one optimised and driving the levers of vitality, choice and joy. I've seen it many times and can tell you this: it feels terrific.

I've learned something important from helping many people plan a successful retirement and from chatting with dozens and dozens of experts in all aspects of retirement: time passes; it is an unstoppable force. Wherever you find yourself today, the simple passing of time means everyone is heading for one of two places. And I do mean everyone. This applies whether you're planning to retire in two months or two years, or even further into the future. Keep this in mind when planning for your later life.

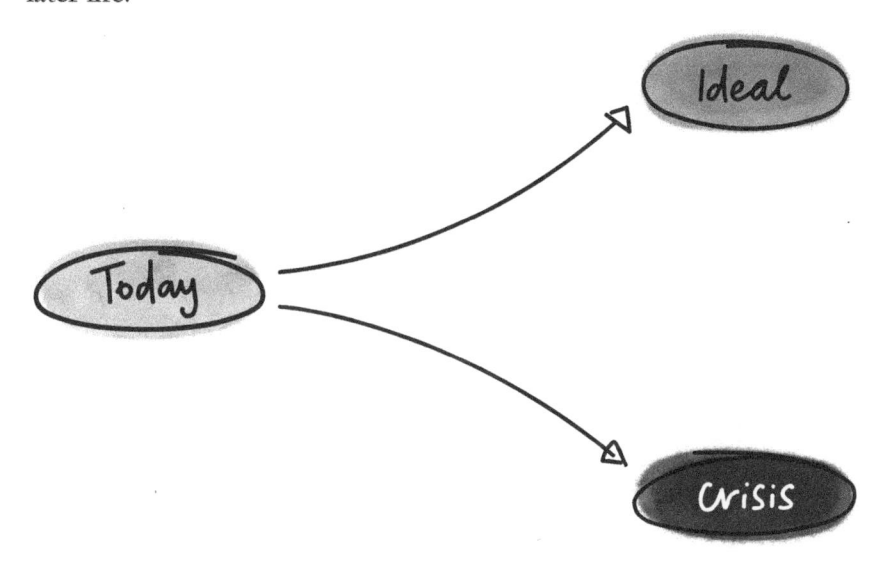

You could reach the highest possible level, in the coveted **ideal** zone – which, of course, is where I want you to end up – having an ideal retirement, a truly fulfilling retirement. Alternatively, there are people who find themselves in a place they really don't want to be – in **crisis**.

Many people think the pathway from where they are today to where they want to be in the future is a straight line. It's not. It's a curve. The line towards crisis in 12 months or 10 years accelerates down and away more rapidly as time goes on. And this occurs because of drift. Drift always takes you downwards.

The curve towards an ideal retirement accelerates up and away more rapidly as time goes on, and as success builds on success.

The key factors here are **decision** and **action**.

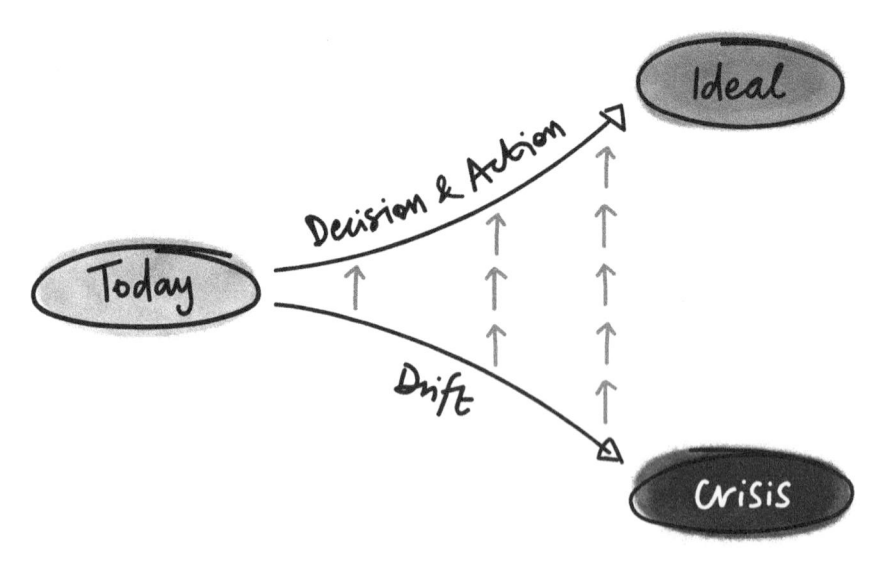

You can see, the difference between being on the bottom line (towards crisis) or the top line (to the highest possible level of retirement success) is the difference between people who allow themselves to drift towards retirement and those who are decisive and make choices.

So the first question to ask yourself is, are you on the decision line?

Are you confident you're heading towards your ideal retirement and later life?

Chapter 14

Now, it becomes pretty obvious that jumping from where you are right now to having your ideal retirement just gets riskier, harder and costlier the longer you wait. As time passes, the gap gets bigger. In fact, in 12 months' or 5 years' time, that jump may be impossible to make. The truth is, that even though that top line might feel like it's a long way away from you right now, it's also as close as it's ever going to be.

Let's assume you're on the top line and you've set a course towards a successful retirement. The second question to ask yourself then is, are you riding the curve? Riding the curve is the process of applying a trusted, proven framework to retirement planning over and over again to give you confidence you're on track for the retirement you deserve.

It's about having a purpose for this stage of life and creating a plan that's right for you. Riding the curve is about looking after yourself so you have the vitality to make choices about your retirement that bring you joy. This means checking in on the continual small decisions and actions you take in the lead-up to, and throughout, your retirement that bring a sense of comfort and reassurance.

So the real question is, how long are you prepared to wait – or how long can you afford to wait – before you take positive, structured action to secure the future you know you can have?

CHAPTER 15

Become the hero of your retirement story

If you're having trouble imagining what your ideal retirement will look like, you could try a slightly different technique. It's a surprisingly helpful tool that might seem a little strange at first.

Inverting the problem is one of dozens of mental models used by billionaire investors Warren Buffett and Charlie Munger. Charlie believes that many hard problems are best solved when they're addressed backwards. When approaching an issue, he is well known for saying, "Invert, always invert." For Charlie and other supporters of this idea, it's not enough to think about challenging problems just one way; you need to think about them both forwards and backwards. To invert the problem – turn it upside down and look at it backwards. By looking at it from a different angle, you're often able to uncover hidden beliefs about the problem you're trying to solve.

In trying to understand how businesses become big and strong, Charlie first studies how businesses decline and die. To understand how to be happy in life, he starts by studying how to make life miserable.

So what does that mean for you? How do you invert the problem of planning a successful retirement?

Sitting down and trying to brainstorm what would make for an ideal, fulfilling retirement can be difficult. You might come up with a bucket list of things you'd like to do, but are you missing some fundamental aspects that could make all the difference to your later years?

So here's what to do – instead of asking yourself what an ideal retirement would look like, ask, what would make a really rubbish, miserable retirement?

Write down all the things you can think of.

Maybe never seeing your children or grandchildren would be on that list. Maybe it would be feeling like you have no purpose, or that you're a burden on others. Maybe it would be dying two days after you retire. What are all the things that would make for a really terrible retirement for you? This process of thinking backwards can really help you avoid obvious pitfalls. It's called 'subtractive avoidance' or 'inversion', and it works to help you avoid trouble. You could think of it as the 'avoiding stupidity' filter, which feels harsh, but if you've identified the possible pitfalls, then you've got a better chance of avoiding them, by planning for success with them in mind.

Figuring what you want, or don't want, out of retirement is a vital exercise, but it really is just the start. Turning vision into reality is not always so straightforward and can feel more than a little overwhelming because when it comes to planning your ideal retirement, it can feel like the system is against you. And in some ways, it is. Modern society hasn't caught up with the needs of an ageing population yet, which is why you need to take control and steer your own path through retirement.

You've taken the first step by reading this book. You have the knowledge; it's now time to put it into action. I've seen my clients make their dream retirement a reality, and I know you can do it too.

Although the road to living your ultimate retirement may be a little bumpy at times, amazing things often follow a little turbulence, but I want you to know that you don't have to weather every storm alone. Come back to this book when you need it and reach out for help. Throughout these chapters, we have seen time and again the importance of community and connection in achieving a truly fulfilling retirement, whatever that looks like for you. John Donne's famous adage, 'No man is an island', doesn't stop being relevant when you step into this next stage of life; in fact, it's more important than ever.

Maybe you are fortunate enough to have lived a wonderful life until now. Perhaps you've climbed to the top of the ladder in your chosen career, been rewarded handsomely both financially and in status and admiration, and enjoyed the fruits of your labour with those you love. What more could retirement possibly offer you?

I would encourage you to consider author David Brooks' perspective that there is a second mountain to be scaled in life, arguably one that offers greater meaning than the first mountain you scaled, which was characterised by a search for career wins, high status and nice things. In his book *The Second Mountain: The Quest for a Moral Life*, David suggests we look towards family, vocation, philosophy and community in retirement to find personal fulfilment and create a life of meaning and purpose.

Your retirement can and should be some of the best years of your life. It's a time full of potential, opportunity and new adventures, if you want it to be. I'm truly excited for you and all the possibilities that lie ahead.

So go for it. Take the next step with confidence and go live the retirement of your dreams.

RESOURCES FOR YOUR RETIREMENT

Chapter 5: Redefining retirement

Bolder. A website on a mission to change perceptions of growing older by sharing stories of inspirational people over 70: www.be-bolder.com

Chapter 6: Having a purpose

Rest Less. A digital community offering career, money, learning and lifestyle advice for over-50s: www.restless.co.uk

Next-Up. Programmes, resources and workshops for planning your retirement transition: www.next-up.com

Chapter 7: It's never too late

Silverfit. A charity promoting happy, healthier ageing through activity programmes that promote physical well-being and social connection: www.silverfit.org.uk

Advantages of Age. An online platform that challenges stereotypes around age: www.advantagesofage.com

Startup School for Seniors. Startup business support and courses for people over 50: www.startupschoolforseniors.com

The Open University. Distance learning courses and adult education: www.open.ac.uk

Now Teach. A charity supporting people who want to start teaching as a second career: www.nowteach.org.uk

Chapter 9: Taking control of your health and well-being

Move it or Lose it! In-person and online fitness classes for older people: www.moveitorloseit.co.uk

The Joy Club. A membership site offering discounts on a wide variety of activities, enabling people to have a joyful and social retirement: www.thejoyclub.com

MenoHealth. Online programmes and exercise classes to support people through the menopause and beyond: www.menohealth.co.uk

Menopausal Mermaids. Facebook group for an informal group of sea swimmers in County Antrim: www.facebook.com/groups/2258310034422870

The Silver Line. A 24/7 telephone support service providing information, friendship and advice to older people: www.thesilverline.org.uk

companiions. An online service that allows people to find support, assistance and company for themselves or their loved ones, helping them stay connected: www.companiions.com

Chapter 10: The Big D

Alzheimer's Society. A charity supporting people affected by dementia: www.alzheimers.org.uk

Music for Dementia. A charity focused on raising awareness and understanding of the role of music in dementia care: www.musicfordementia.org.uk

Comentis. Helping organisations to proactively identify and triage 'at-risk' clients: www.comentis.co.uk/LastingPowerofAttorney

How to make, register or end a lasting power of attorney: www.gov.uk/power-of-attorney

Friends Against Scams. National Trading Standards Scams Team initiative protecting and preventing people from becoming victims of scams: www.friendsagainstscams.org.uk

Action Fraud. 24/7 reporting platform for fraud and cyber crime: www.actionfraud.police.uk

Citizens Advice. A confidential advice service: www.citizensadvice.org.uk

Chapter 11: Planning for a 30-year retirement

Office for National Statistics. To calculate your life expectancy: www.ons.gov.uk

State Pension forecast. www.gov.uk/check-state-pension

The Good Funeral Guide. A not-for-profit organisation providing information and advice about organising a funeral: www.goodfuneralguide.co.uk

Settld. A free death notification service to inform private sector companies in one go: www.settld.care

Tell Us Once. A free death notification service to inform government companies in one go: www.gov.uk/after-a-death/organisations-you-need-to-contact-and-tell-us-once

Chapter 13: Care and the end of life

My Care Consultant. An independent service to help you plan and arrange long-term care: www.mycareconsultant.co.uk

Death Cafe. National and international informal meetings for people who want to talk about death: www.deathcafe.com

Compassion in Dying. A free information line, publications and resources to help people plan and prepare for the end of life: www.compassionindying.org.uk

My Decisions. A free online tool to help you record an advance decision and an advance statement: www.mydecisions.org.uk

RECOMMENDED READING

Chapter 5: Redefining retirement

The 100-Year Life: Living and Working in an Age of Longevity by Lynda Gratton and Andrew J Scott (Bloomsbury)

How to Age Joyfully: Eight Steps to a Happier, Fuller Life by Maggy Pigott (Vie Books)

Generation Cherry by Tim Drake (RedDoor Publishing)

Chapter 6: Having a purpose

Not Fade Away: How to Thrive in Retirement by Celia Dodd (Green Tree)

A Golden Civilization & the Map of Mindfulness by George Kinder (Serenity Point Press)

Alchemy: The Magic of Original Thinking in a World of Mind-Numbing Conformity by Rory Sutherland (W H Allen)

Chapter 7: It's never too late

Irongran: How Keeping Fit Taught Me That Growing Older Needn't Mean Slowing Down by Edwina Brocklesby (Sphere)

Chapter 8: The science of living better for longer

Sod 70!: The Guide to Living Well by Muir Gray (Bloomsbury)

Sod Sitting, Get Moving!: Getting Active in Your 60s, 70s and Beyond by Diana Moran and Muir Gray (Green Tree)

Successful Aging: A Neuroscientist Explores the Power and Potential of Our Lives by Daniel J. Levitin (E P Dutton)

Chapter 9: Taking control of your health and well-being

The Psychology of Exercise by Josephine Perry (Routledge)

Never Too Old To Lift: 8 Steps to Create Your First 12-Week Strength Training Program by Chris Tiley (Independently published)

Dead Man Running: One Man's Story of Running to Stay Alive by Kevin Webber (Pitch Publishing)

Chapter 10: The Big D

Increase Your Brainability—And Reduce Your Risk of Dementia by Charles Alessi, Larry W. Chambers and Muir Gray (Oxford University Press)

The 'D' Word: Rethinking Dementia by Mary Jordan and Noel Collins (Hammersmith Health Books)

Grandpa on a Skateboard: The practicalities of assessing mental capacity and unwise decisions by Tim Farmer (Rethink Press)

Chapter 12: The role of investing

The Bogle Effect: How John Bogle and Vanguard Turned Wall Street Inside Out and Saved Investors Trillions by Eric Balchunas (Matt Holt)

Invest Your Way to Financial Freedom: A Simple Guide to Everything You Need to Know by Ben Carlson and Robin Powell (Harriman House Publishing)

Triumph of the Optimists: 101 Years of Global Investment Returns by Elroy Dimson (Princeton University Press)

The Intelligent Investor: The Definitive Book on Value Investing by Benjamin Graham (HarperBus)

Chapter 13: Care and the end of life

End of Life: The Essential Guide for Carers by Mary Jordan and Judy Carole Kauffmann (Hammersmith Press)

Chapter 15: Become the hero of your retirement story

The Second Mountain: The Quest for a Moral Life by David Brooks (Allen Lane)